HEALING through the
AKASHIC RECORDS

Additional Works by Linda Howe

How to Read the Akashic Records:
Accessing the Archive of the Soul and Its Journey

Healing Through the Akashic Records:
Guided Practices for Using the Power of Your Sacred Wounds
to Discover Your Soul's Perfection (audio)

How to Read the Akashic Records:
Accessing the Archive of the Soul and Its Journey (audio)

HEALING through the
AKASHIC
RECORDS

Using the Power of
Your Sacred Wounds
to Discover Your
Soul's Perfection

LINDA HOWE

SOUNDS TRUE

BOULDER, COLORADO

Sounds True, Inc., Boulder CO 80306

Published 2011

Book design by Lisa Kerans
Cover image based on an illustration by Vilnis Lauzums, available at shutterstock.com

An excerpt from the Twenty-Third Psalm on page vii comes from an 1885 edition of the Bible, King James version, revised.

Printed in Canada

Library of Congress Cataloging-in-Publication Data

Howe, Linda, 1954-
    Healing through the Akashic records : using the power of your sacred wounds to discover your soul's perfection / Linda Howe.
        p. cm.
    ISBN 978-1-60407-096-5
    1. Akashic records. 2. Mental healing. 3. Parapsychology. I. Title.

    BF1045.A44H67 2011
    133.9—dc22
                                            2010037874

10 9 8 7 6 5 4 3

eBook ISBN 978-1-60407-333-1

To Lisa and Michael.
You are my favorite traveling companions.
I love you both.

Yea, though I walk through the valley of the shadow of death,
I will fear no evil,
For Thou art with me;

Surely goodness and mercy shall follow me all the days of my life.

—*Psalm 23*

Contents

Preface: A Healing Journey

In my first book, *How to Read the Akashic Records,* I described the winding path that led me to the Records. It began with a fervent prayer. I pleaded with God to tell me how it could be that my perfectly fine life—success in school, a good job, a nice apartment—had left me feeling perfectly miserable. My prayer was answered almost immediately, and in a way I could never have anticipated. This did not come in the form of an answer to my question; instead, I entered into a state of utter stillness. And then, without my having wished for it or even considered such a thing, I had a direct and profound experience of oneness, of the unbreakable connection between myself and all other things, seen and unseen. For the first time in my life, I felt relief from my ever-present internal distress.

I now *knew* without doubt that God existed, and I could feel that God knew, loved, and even *liked* me just as I was. The experience lasted only a few moments, but it was a revelation.

Then those moments passed, and that brief taste of God propelled me to search further. I wanted to reclaim the experience in order to heal the deep emotional wounds I had been suffering seemingly forever. First, I sought God in traditional places: in churches and temples. Next, I immersed myself in the archetypal symbolism of the tarot. Then one day I found myself—reluctantly, I must admit—sitting in a shamanic drumming circle, and despite myself, I was entranced, transported to another dimension. After that experience, I dove headlong into the teachings and rituals of shamanism. But it was not until I was introduced to the Akashic Records that I truly came home: home to my soul and my own true Self.

This was where my personal story ended in my last book—I followed it only with a brief account of how I came to be a teacher of the Akashic Records and how my teaching system evolved. But there is much more to my tale. I have chosen to share some of it with you now in greater depth because it is intertwined with the healing system you are about to learn. In fact, this program of healing through the Akashic Records arose from my personal healing journey.

It began when I opened my own Records for the very first time. I had heard others describe their experience—I was intrigued and eager to learn how to do it myself. Thus I now sat in a room with a few other students, following the teacher's direction, anticipating with excitement what it was going to be like to open my Records—if, that is, I could accomplish it at all. I had an impression of the Records as a highly esoteric, sophisticated oracle, and I imagined a dramatic experience at the very instant my own Records opened: a riot of phenomena and sensation. Perhaps an electric crackling in my ears. Lights flashing in otherworldly colors. Maybe even a thundering voice from beyond.

Then, unexpectedly, the teacher's voice grew faint. My attention turned inward and I could hear my own inner voice: the teacher within. All became still—my mind's chatter and the turmoil of my emotions hung suspended. Within the profound quiet that remained, I knew peace, clarity, safety, and love. I felt wave upon wave of relief … until I was simply overcome.

And I knew without a doubt that my search for the right spiritual path had ended.

♦

The next stage of my spiritual development now lay open before me. I had found a way to contact an infinite resource that could guide my spiritual practice, and so I embarked upon a sacred journey of healing. For the next sixteen years, I worked diligently in my own Records, finding solutions to lifelong problems and cultivating my growth.

Though I had spent considerable time searching elsewhere, from that first experience I had great hope that I had finally arrived at a way to cross the spiritual desert in which I had been wandering and achieve a deep level of healing. It had shown up in my life not a moment too soon: I badly needed help. I needed to find ways to overcome my fear and agitation. I had to learn how to stop being so dependent upon others for approval and support. I needed to grow in spiritual maturity until I was solid enough—secure enough in myself—that I could receive from others. Ultimately, I had to find a way to reliably connect with the Divine Energy within so I could relax and truly enjoy my life.

I had always needed exactly *this* kind of resilient spirituality to help me move through my life and cope with challenges large and small. A spirituality that would enable me to stay true to myself, be strong, and participate in life. The Akashic Records seemed to offer me all of this, and as the work unfolded, their promise was realized. No matter what problem I worked through at any given time, my Records never failed me.

I did not set out to develop a system of healing to share; I had only one aim: to heal myself. Along the way—without my even noticing at first—an entire healing program was revealed to me. A slim sliver at a time: useful insights, exercises I could practice, other kinds of "homework" to do, and suggestions for appropriate action. A two-step system of listening and acting assembled itself one puzzle piece at a time, and it wasn't until it was largely complete that I was able to take in the whole of it and comprehend what I had. Indeed, a system had emerged from my work in the Records that brought about my own healing, and, I suspected, had the power to benefit many others.

But, I did not recognize this for some time. Working in the Records, I focused entirely upon myself: my issues, my pain, my struggles, and my search for *practical* solutions. I had had many intense spiritual experiences before, so at first the Records' emphasis on practical wisdom seemed strange.

But useful ideas, suggestions, and strategies were exactly what I needed to sustain myself while navigating everyday life. If I couldn't apply spiritual insights to my daily experience, I concluded, what good were they to me? So this became my bottom line: the direction I received from the Records had to *work*. It had to be trustworthy. The guidance had to be reasonable. I had to be able to rely upon this guidance in any circumstance. Every element, every insight and tool I received had to contribute something of substance to my healing journey.

At first, I applied the guidance from the Records simply because it rang true. Then, time after time, I noticed that it was exactly what I needed. Each time I applied what I learned and took to heart the suggestions received, I felt better. These new insights led to sensible, doable actions that produced consistently positive results. This happened countless times and in ways large and small. Carrying the awareness of the Divine gained through the Akashic Records into the everydayness of my life, I began to mature spiritually.

It has been a dance of discovery. Initially, I concentrated a great deal of my energy on the method I used to access the Records (the Pathway Prayer Process to Access the Heart of the Akashic Records, described in chapter 3). But as I came into relationship with my own spiritual authority, my emphasis shifted from the method of access to the insights, guidance, and wisdom such access afforded.

For a glimpse of how the guidance of the Records can manifest, I will share with you one of my deepest healing experiences: one that had a direct impact on several of those closest to me as well.

My father's death was a slow and terribly painful one. Perhaps you, too, have been helpless in the face of a loved one's suffering. The compassionate space of the Records gave me relief from the sadness and angst I experienced during that trying time, and this in itself was a tremendous healing gift.

But I remained troubled. I felt tied in knots about how my siblings should respond: both to my father's care and to handling the emotionally wrenching situation themselves. (There were knots tied within knots tied within knots—I am the second child of eight!) I was certain I knew what each of my brothers and sisters should do, and I felt strongly compelled to manage and direct their actions. As you might imagine, my direction was not always welcome.

The Records revealed a different approach. They led me to an understanding that all of my brothers and sisters were entitled to their own experience of our father's death. They showed me that not only was it inappropriate for me to guide, urge, or try to inspire my siblings—for I truly did not know what was best for them—it was also unnecessary. I came to understand that each of us had a unique relationship with our father and that it was insulting and demeaning of me to force my perceptions on another.

This was not an easy realization to come to: none of us wants to discover that our behavior has been insulting or demeaning. But it was revealed to me over time and with compassion. Whenever I felt an impending "attack" of the need to direct my siblings' behavior, I went to work in the Records, and gradually I was relieved of the fears underlying this unexpectedly strong urge. I came to know and trust that everyone could take care of him- or herself. The first time I brought this problem to the Records, the knots began to soften. The next time, they slackened further. At last, they dissolved altogether, ultimately yielding to a sense of peace.

This invaluable discovery—that each one of my siblings had his or her own rightful pathway through our father's death—is one I cannot now unlearn. It is with me always. This is what I mean by growing in spiritual maturity.

◆

From this example you can see that, while the Akashic Records contain many wonderful gifts for healing, working in them can be uncomfortable at times. This was especially true for me at first. As I engaged with the Records, I was flying blind—and often alone. I did not have the benefit of my own hindsight or anyone else's. Yes, some incredible people were placed on my path to assist me in navigating certain stretches, but no one accompanied me the entire way. No one could tell me how it would all turn out. I pressed onward in what often felt like darkness, following just enough inner light to take the next step without falling.

Gradually, however, I developed a relationship with the Divine Presence within—one that is rewarding beyond measure—and life is no longer such a struggle. I have come to trust that part of myself through repeated experience: through a regular practice of going within, seeking guidance, applying the counsel I receive, taking action, and observing the results. Through trial and error, I have learned to recognize and trust the presence of the Divine, or God. And I have learned that this trust is at the heart of the healing power of the Akashic Records.

My story still unfolds, day by day, as I live my now extraordinarily ordinary life. As this spiritual healing program has evolved, I have made many discoveries. The most important is that the Divine Presence is real. There is a power greater than me, and it is both within me and beyond me. Having a conscious relationship with this power makes all the difference in the quality of my daily life and in my relationships with my family, my friends, and myself. This is precious knowledge I have gained—quite unexpectedly—through my explorations of the Akashic Records.

Today, my connection to the essence of the Light of the Akasha, the pulse of Life, the Divine Reality, is solid. I know this Light has been with me always: awake or asleep, at times of ease and times of hardship, whether I feel pain or pleasure, whether I get what I want or not. It is alive and it is resilient—and it is healing me. My awareness of the Divine is continually enhanced by my work in the Records, and I know it will further strengthen with continued practice. Of this I am absolutely certain. It is my heartfelt desire and intention that you, too, will experience deep connection and healing through the wisdom and guidance of the Akashic Records. And so I now share this healing system with you.

Acknowledgments

I am continually blessed with support, seen and unseen. To the unseen, I extend my heartfelt gratitude for my life and for the gift of awareness.

To the seen, I offer an enthusiastic *"Thank You!"*

To the inspiring, heroic, compassionate students who have joined me on the path, know that you have made my journey rich beyond measure.

This particular project brought together some truly wonderful people. A special thank you to Linda Joy Stone and Janis Portugal for helping me get started. Thanks to Karen Low for courageously offering just the assistance I needed, and for being so good-natured throughout. To Rachel Guy, thank you for taking care of loose ends and laughing at my jokes. Thanks to Anne Horrigan for sharing your wicked wit and hilarious insights. To Amy Sczepaniak, a special thank you for your kindness and clear thinking. Dawn Silver and Shelia Leidy deserve eternal thanks for their sisterhood.

To Susan Lucci, I offer my deepest gratitude for your clarity, commitment, vision, and nerves of steel. Thank you for holding steady and true to a high standard of excellence and being a generous genius. Words are inadequate to express my appreciation to Jean Lachowicz, the incredible wonder woman. Your loyalty, dedication, understanding, and patience are amazing. Thank you for your brilliance and fierce protection. You are the best.

I am truly blessed to have you all in my life as travelers on the path and, more important, as my friends. Thank you all.

To a person, those I have encountered at Sounds True are impeccable. What good fortune for me to be able to work with this group of talented and generous folks. Thank you all so very much. Finally, to Sheridan McCarthy: Thank you for helping me discover the value of my work.

Introduction

I am so glad you have found your way to this book. The simple fact that you have arrived here says a lot about you and where you are in your life journey. Something inside of you—a nudge from your soul—is guiding you to know that *now* is the time to advance on your healing quest to become the person you are meant to be and to live a life you love.

When the soul says it's time, it's time. You have both the ability and the wisdom to hear this prompting from your Innermost Self, and you have the good sense to act on it. This is fabulous!

In your hands is a guide to a path of spiritual healing that is extraordinarily practical and effective—and remarkably simple. It has led me out of a crushing sense of isolation and into a conscious relationship with the Divine Presence. This is a very specific healing practice, as the title indicates: we work in the Akashic Records, using the wounds we have suffered during our lives as the means to come to know our true selves, to discover our soul's perfection.

This approach came to me piece by piece over a sixteen-year period when I was striving to be more authentic, closer to myself, and to more fully enjoy my connections with the people in my life. I was also looking for ways in which I could contribute value to life without getting tangled up in all the world's chaos. The healing program that developed over time answered all these needs. Here was a way for me to grow into greater trust in the goodness of life so I could truly let go of outdated ways of operating and discover new, more appropriate habits. I found a method that supported my heartfelt desire to let go of the illusion of control, surrendering to the benevolent power of life and allowing this force for good to transform all the dimensions of my being.

I discovered this path of radical change by using the Akashic Records as an empowering spiritual practice. As I followed the guidance I found there, my wounds were transformed from obstacles to knowing myself, others, and the joy of life into means of connection. What most astonished me about my discoveries was that *through* my difficulties—not despite them—I encountered the Divine Presence in a very real way. I came to know that nothing could possibly happen to me that could ever corrupt or destroy the Divine spark within me. I discovered that the connection I have with the Divine, and with life itself, is unshakable. And now, standing firmly on the foundation of this knowledge, I am secure enough to build a life that expresses the best truths of who I am.

I have since taught this method to hundreds of other people through classes, workshops, and one-on-one sessions, and I have seen firsthand that each individual who earnestly undertakes its practices achieves healing. Some stories are dramatic—complete reversals of debilitating conditions. Others are subtler: emergence of a greater sense of self-confidence and well-being, an improvement in a key relationship. Everyone who approaches this path with intention and openness experiences some measure of positive change: transformation of a condition from which they have long sought relief, or an opening into the joy of life. I have seen no exceptions.

The key is facing, from a spiritual perspective, the source of our pain and distress: wounds we have inevitably incurred throughout our lives, beginning in infancy, that affect us to the present day. Through working in the Akashic Records, we change our relationship to these wounds. Examining them in the Light of the Akasha, we come to view all the hurt we have experienced—all the damage inflicted upon us by ourselves and others—as sacred opportunities for transformation and avenues to encounter the Divine Reality. They are exactly that, as you will soon discover. While we incur them at the mundane level of everyday life on earth, they have a higher purpose. Our human experiences are the crucible within which we encounter the indestructible Divine Essence that is the very core of our being.

If you are drawn to this book, chances are good that you have already pursued healing in other ways. You have invested time, money, and energy in gaining relief from your present discomfort, whether it is physical, emotional, or mental in nature, or a combination. The knowledge and understanding you gained through your efforts have likely been helpful to you, but probably not transformational: some discomfort remains, whether acute or mild. This is not because you are lazy, or don't deserve relief from pain and distress, or you somehow want difficulty in your life. It simply means that you have run up against the limits of your abilities as a human to find solutions. Transforming your woundedness requires freedom from limitation, and to achieve this you need access to the infinite nature of the realm of spiritual power.

Spiritual healing differs from all other modalities in that it results directly from strengthening our relationship with the Divine. We accomplish this by initiating, and then consciously and continually developing, an intimate relationship with our Innermost Self, a facet of our soul. Our soul never loses sight of its oneness with Divine Nature; our Innermost Self serves as our own personal bridge to the Divine.

As a result of our wounding, it appears we have lost touch with this deepest part of ourselves and hence our soul. But no matter how distant we may seem to be from our soul, we are in fact inseparable from it. Futhermore, the soul remains an infinite resource for healing. Our challenge is to clear away the distorted filters of long-established patterns of wounded thoughts and feelings that keep us from knowing the Innermost Self and, in turn, the Divine. This is the essence of our work in the Records. It is important to note that, while this deep work takes place in the spiritual realm, it is simultaneously entirely practical. Through clarifying our difficulties, gaining insights into them, and arriving at real-world solutions, we can bring this work into our everyday lives. We become reacquainted with the truest aspect of ourselves, the Innermost Self.

In this process for healing, we recognize we have an important part to play: taking responsibility for our well-being and doing what we can to care for ourselves. What remains is the part we really cannot accomplish on our own, and here we allow the Divine to move on our behalf. This method guides us to a safe place within which we are sufficiently supported and where we can allow this force for transformational good to be exactly that. We are entitled to experience the perfection of our own soul, and this strategy for healing enables us to encounter the essence of our Divine Nature. When this happens, we find that we are the person we always hoped we could be and we can now live the life that we've always dreamed possible.

Prerequisites for Healing Through the Akashic Records

There are just two prerequisites for healing through the Akashic Records. First, we must recognize the futility of applying the same old ideas to our problems and come to accept that what we have been trying has not worked. Second, we need to have a sense—and in the beginning it can be a mere wisp of a sense—that it is safe to let go of the old ways and open ourselves to the new, because there exists a power for healing that is far greater than we are.

The beauty of the Akashic Records, as you will learn, is that they are an environment organized expressly to provide the safety needed so we can encounter the Divine presence in a way that is real, absolutely useful, and decidedly effective.

The Three Components of Our Healing Adventure

Our healing journey is divided into three main parts. The first phase is Our Sacred Wounds as Points of Power in Our Relationship with Ourselves. In this phase, we address the devastating problems of self-abandonment and self-rejection from the following significant points of view: Awareness of Self, Self-Acceptance, Appropriate Action, and Choice. Exploring this stage of the healing process, we find ways to stay with ourselves no matter what is happening in life and to be at peace even during trying times. Finding the wounds that have made it virtually impossible to make contact with our Innermost Self is in fact the precise opening needed to enter into its depths.

Next we examine Our Sacred Wounds as a Pathway to Peace in Our Relations with Others. This is a very exciting part of our journey. We are given the opportunity to find out how to move beyond resentment of others and into acceptance and forgiveness—and to examine what is required to cease negative judgments. The great challenge of disrupting limiting patterns follows. We are given the opportunity to discover the life cycle of patterns and transition from being enslaved by them to becoming free and empowered—and see that the difficulties that interrupt the connection between us are exactly what we will use as the path of peace in relationships.

Finally, we enter into the region of Our Sacred Wounds as a Platform for Transformation and Transcendence. Having completed our work in the first two phases, we find ourselves more solid, stable, and better able to express our true Self. But we are not through yet. We are infinite beings on an eternal quest. In spiritual work, there is always more, always a next level and a next step. In this stage of our healing work, we establish a conscious relationship with our internal structure through which we thrive in a renewed life, one lived beyond human wounds and scars. I will introduce to you the Ascension Matrix, which provides a context through which you can experience transcendence into a more conscious fusion with the Divine. The elements of the Matrix are Gratitude, Grace, and Generosity. Here, we come to know how to activate each of these qualities in life and live as an ascending being. And we discover how to live in the world, not as a victim of it, but as both active participant and inspired contributor. We will learn how to live our ordinary life from an extraordinary perspective.

Prepare for the Journey

To support you in this three-stage process, I would like to make some suggestions for ways to approach the work. Feel free to accept those that are helpful for you, and don't worry about the rest.

You might want to start by reading quickly through all three sections (parts 2, 3, and 4) and letting yourself get used to the flow of the work before doing any of the exercises. Some sections may be very engaging for you right now, others not so much; this is natural, so let your intuition about this be your guide. You may wish to dedicate a special notebook and pen to sharing what arises as you work in your Records. In each of the three sections, I introduce ideas and discuss possibilities for applying them in your life, and I will present tried-and-true questions for reflection to take into your Akashic Records. Feel free to work with them at your own pace and follow where they lead. Experiment, experiment, experiment to see how to best interact with them for your own growth.

You will begin by learning to access your Records using the Pathway Prayer Process to Access the Heart of the Akashic Records. If you are already familiar with this, it will be a good review. If you are new to the work, this is the basic instruction required to open your Akashic Records and begin working in them. For a more detailed presentation of how to do this, you might wish to explore my book *How to Read the Akashic Records.* Some people enjoy gaining a deeper understanding of the method, but it is not essential to do so before using the Pathway Prayer for these purposes. The instruction here will be enough to get you started.

Before you commence working in the Records, I suggest you take a few minutes to reflect upon those difficulties that have been with you as long as you can remember. Turn your attention to those issues that just do not seem to budge— ones you have been chiseling away at for perhaps the last ten, twenty, or even thirty years. Another approach is to go straight to the thorniest places: to reflect upon the most painful experiences or ways of being you have been enduring, those that cause such intense discomfort that you usually refuse to even let yourself think about them. I understand that neither of these exercises is easy—we all have had ample practice attempting to escape our wounds and relatively little experience facing them directly. But you can do it, knowing help is coming: the solace, perspective, and wisdom you will find in your Akashic Records. Trust me, I have traveled this road to spiritual healing many, many times before you, and I have written this book as a way to "leave the lights on" for you, to guide you on your way.

I know how hard it is to live with hurt feelings and the scar tissue that has built up around them. I know how difficult it is to be held hostage to old patterns of interacting with others. I know how demoralizing it is to keep trying to change but to fail again and again. And I know what it is like to use your shortcomings against yourself. It is because I have suffered these experiences too, and have been relieved of them, that I am sharing this method with you. Believe me: your efforts will bring tremendous liberation.

An Invitation

Now I would like to extend to you a formal invitation to begin this three-stage journey of liberation. Wherever you are on your path, come along. I will be with you every step of the way. I will fully explain everything you need to understand as you move through a progression of healing concepts and methods that will absolutely transform your life.

This is an invitation to become free to know the truth about your Innermost Self and to express it in the world. It's an invitation to surrender to the Divine and into the joy of living. I invite you to open your mind, soften your heart, and align with your will so the Light of Akasha can move to you, through you, and into the world around you. Wherever you now find yourself, know that your next level of possibility, your next dimension of wholeness, wellness, and aliveness is in front of you. Spiritual healing is within your reach.

PART ONE

The Fundamentals

CHAPTER ONE

An Introduction to the Akashic Records

The Akashic Records are a healing realm made up of *Akasha:* the primary substance. This substance is Light, the essential life force as it exists before our thoughts and feelings step in to manipulate it. It is both a presence and a healing force. Nonintrusive by nature, the Akashic Records never impose themselves upon us. They never interfere with our choices, even under the most desperate of circumstances: they do not compromise human dignity. Instead, the energy of the Records *responds* to our desire for assistance, to the cry of our heart when we are in pain. When we are open to the energy of the Akasha—even just a little—it moves toward us to meet our needs. It approaches at a pace we can manage, one that supports us and is not frightening.

At its most basic, our task when working with the Records is to become aligned with ourselves. Once we are centered, we can then direct our attention to the Light and let it do the work.

A Superior Intelligence

One of the assumptions we make in this work is that the Light of the Akasha is an intelligence superior to our own. It is infinite knowledge and wisdom. It is the Light of the mind of God moving through the heart of the energy body of God. And because it is a greater intelligence, we do not have to tell it what to do: we trust that it operates on our behalf and for our own good. As I have observed repeatedly through years of teaching and my own experience, the more we experiment with the Light, the more positive results we see and the better we are able to trust the actions of the Light. The more we trust, the more Light we can allow, and the more we allow, the more frequently and quickly the Light moves on our behalf.

Spiritual Healing Through the Akashic Records

Spiritual healing can be defined generally as *healing from the point of view of the soul.* Let's take a look at the qualities and dynamics of the spiritual healing process that are specific to the Akashic Records.

An Atmosphere of Transformation

The principles governing the Records establish and maintain an encouraging atmosphere for transformation. There is a predictable, progressive pattern to the flow of Akashic energy that operates at every level, and there are energy dynamics at work in our relationship with the Akasha that facilitate change.

An infinite spiritual resource, the Akashic Records are a dimension of consciousness that contains the vibrational record of every soul and its journey. There are two components to each individual's set of Records: the fixed and the evolving. The fixed aspect is the essential pattern of your soul, which can be understood as the DNA of *who you are at the level of your soul.* More importantly, this is the soul-level truth about you: who you truly are in your human journey through time and space. The second part of your set of Records is the *lifetimes you experience as you become aware of the essence of yourself.* Here you find the ever-evolving catalog of the human experiences you have had, are having, and will continue to have, as you move toward awakening.

We Are Allowers of Healing

When we work within the Akashic Records, we are "allowers" of healing. As we align with ourselves and our truth, the Light does the work. We do not send energy to our Records or receive energy from them; in the Records, we recognize that the Light within us is within everyone and everything, so there is no reason to send or receive. Our challenge is to allow the Light to move through us. We do this by "cleaning house," making more inner space so that what is already present can be revealed. We take stock of our own makeup and let go of anything that interferes with our ability to experience our own goodness. As we engage in this process, we free up room within our interior for the ever-present Light to expand. The Light supports our housecleaning, corrects any imbalances we may have, and quickens our ability to be happy and joyful.

Some environments are more conducive to such a healing experience than others. The atmosphere within the Akashic Records is highly supportive of transformation, and this is because of the essential principles that govern the Records.

"Judge Not," "Fear Not," and "Resist Not" are the absolutes of the Akasha. In combination, these principles produce a culture of honor, kindness, and respect, providing us with an opportunity to know our own souls as whole, complete, and good. As we gain this knowledge, we transform. We shift from being judgmental, fearful, and resistant to becoming accepting, allowing, and embracing. When we examine our difficulties from within the Akashic domain and its governing principles, we see our problems as they truly are. As many of us have learned, once revealed, the truth sets us free.

The influence of the "Judge Not" principle establishes a neutral space where it is easier for us to be honest. In an environment free of judgment, there is no threat of criticism. Free of the potential for judgment and the pressure it creates, we can simply observe and report what we see. Events and situations are no longer perceived as indictments or evidence of our failures; they are simply events and situations. In such a space, it is safe to take a good look at what we have done, or have not done, and know that the Records offer no support for using anything against ourselves.

Adding "Fear Not" to the mix amplifies the benevolent climate of the Akasha. Here we meet the kindness, respect, and high regard that are ever-present for us. Bullying, shame, harassment, and ridicule dissolve in such an atmosphere. "Judge Not" and "Fear Not" are twin principles: if there is no active negative judgment, there is no reason to be afraid. While this comes as a great relief, it can take some getting used to—we are initially unaccustomed to the absence of judgment and fear. Regular exposure to this climate enables us to adjust to the freedom inherent in it, and over time we find that we no longer have to hide or protect ourselves from what is going on within us and around us.

"Resist Not" is the force that enables us to allow, let go, and then move on. If we are blocking or pushing away some aspect of ourselves or our experience, paradoxically it gets wedged into us, and we find ourselves barricaded behind the very thing we do not want. On the other hand, in an atmosphere where there is no harsh judgment, and hence no fear, it is unnecessary to wall ourselves off from our experience. We can simply let go and let life flow. We can adjust ourselves to the natural movement of the life force within and around us and relax into it. In the presence of "Resist Not" energy, we lose our attachment to being stuck. We realize it is safe for us to evolve.

When we are aware of these energetic forces operating within the realm of the Akashic Records, we can sense their great potential to assist us in our transformation. Because the active principles of "Judge Not," "Fear Not," and "Resist Not" are always at work, spiritual healing through the Akashic Records allows us to enter into a very safe space in consciousness, and what is no longer appropriate for us dissolves.

The Formed Word

Understand that in the Akashic Records, energy moves on the formed word: spoken, written, or thought. This is true outside of the Records as well—words always carry great energetic power—but the energy is intensified within them. The movement of energy becomes even more potent within the Records because of both the clarified environment in which an individual forms words as well as the level of attention that she or he pays to their formation. As we speak the truth about any given situation, the energy of that situation shifts and loosens. Whatever we speak about transforms: its energy moves and becomes unstuck, and problems begin to resolve themselves. Simply by describing any given circumstance, even if we do not fully understand it, frozen energy patterns begin to thaw. The "tectonic plates" of the life force, once held rigidly in place, let go, and we come to discover our right relationship with our life, ourselves, and others. Then we can simply let life be, relieved of any torment surrounding past difficulties.

The Journey to Peace

One tantalizing possibility the Akashic Records offer is peace. After we work for some time in the Records, this quality of tranquility moves into the deepest part of who we are—and it stays. We become less likely to take things personally. The floor of our being becomes imbued with peace, and though turbulence may continue to occur, we move in the direction of a more peaceful, less agitated life.

This is not resignation or putting up with harmful conditions, such as "making peace" with a bad situation. I am speaking of a higher-level peace that transcends daily circumstances. We might not get the results we think we need; we might not find the person we believe we must meet to be fulfilled; we might not get the job we feel we require to be happy. We may not attain the level of health we desire or the financial situation we believe we need to attain to feel secure. When it comes to spiritual healing and this quality of peace, we are considering the possibility of being at peace whether things go our way or not. It is easy to feel a sense of peace when we get what we want, but the challenge is to feel at ease either way. When we engage in the Akashic Records and enjoy the atmosphere of kindness and respect we find there, peace becomes progressively easier to achieve.

Working with the Light Grid

Within the culture of the Akashic Records, we find a supportive environment in which we can better see what is happening and make ourselves available for transformation. Here we have access to, and make contact with, the Light Grid that holds and defines who we are.

Surrounding every person is a pattern of points of Light. Each of these points is connected to one another in a resonating relationship based on the emanating frequencies. The Light Grid is an unseen energy that holds us together. The energetic patterns contain who we are. Each of us is the physical manifestation of this unique configuration of points of Light: it is as simple as that. Our Light Grid is immediately—but not directly—accessible in the Records. We influence it through our humanness both within and outside of the Records. Through engaging with our feelings, thoughts, and physical experiences, we transform our corresponding Light Grid.

Clusters of points of Light connect to parts of our human constitution: our bodies, emotions, and thoughts. The human vehicle is the domain through which we can directly encounter the Divine, and the Light Grid is a conduit for expanded awareness of the Divine. Addressing our worldly concerns—health, happiness, family, friends, all the various facets of life—is *the* way to interface effectively with the Grid.

As I mentioned before, when we interact with the Records, we put our experience into words. As we speak, write, or think these words, we affect the Light Grid. As we identify and describe the truth, we change the grid, altering it to accurately represent the current reality. Old, fossilized patterns begin to undo themselves. New constellations of the Grid assemble and find their rightful place within the whole of our energy system. What is happening is an adjustment to the pattern *at the level of the pattern itself.* The reassembled Grid supports us as we interact with this new, more appropriate pattern and have a chance to grow into it.

It's similar to altering a pattern for a garment. At one time in your life, the pattern may have fit perfectly; then, as life progresses, you may notice it tugs or chafes—even causing you discomfort. When you are in the Records, places where the pattern still fits and places where it no longer does are easier to identify, and as you address the situations causing an awkward fit, you can alter the pattern accordingly. The words you use in the Records serve to describe the alterations you need, and the pattern of the Light Grid is then perfectly customized to your specific needs. It becomes much easier for you to change your thoughts, feelings, and behavior than ever before; change is no longer a struggle.

The natural process of healing through the Akashic Records begins with the transformation of the Light Grid patterns holding us in place, acting as energetic containers—parameters for our human expression. Telling the truth about our experience changes the configuration. As the pattern is altered to reflect our current consciousness, we respond and can change the way we operate.

Three Stages of Healing

As you progress on your journey of spiritual healing, you will notice that there is a predictable sequence to the flow of Akashic energy at each stage of development. There are three distinct stages of healing within the Records: the Story, Causes and Conditions, and the Soul Truth.

The Story of What Is Happening

The first level of healing requires discerning *the story of what is happening.* This is the ordinary story of what is taking place for us here and how: something challenging at work, a sudden bout of the flu, an unexpected bonus that opens up new possibilities, disappointment in a friend's behavior, a new romance. These are the stories of our everyday human life. The Akashic Records contain the story of who we are through time and space. Within this system, the story of what is happening to us, around us, and through us *now* is very important. The more specifically we can describe our circumstances, the better, as healing involves the specific, not the general. Begin by describing in detail what has happened or is happening to you and what the experience is like. Identify your role in the matter and how you are affected.

Causes and Conditions

Causes and conditions make up the second stage of healing within the Akashic Records. Here we work at the level of knowledge and understanding. We explore our beliefs about our situation. We examine our thoughts about these circumstances. At this level, we seek to understand what has caused any difficulty. Within the Records, we find that what we are experiencing is anchored in either something from this lifetime or from another—it doesn't matter which. At this level, we can make sense of our problems. Here, we can see environmental factors, past-life influences, and ancestral patterns contributing to a particular dilemma. This is an especially fascinating stage of the healing process, often rich with ideas, insights, and comprehension. It is important to mine this stage for resolution. When the mind attains some sense of understanding it usually then relaxes, freeing us to move beyond the known to where the most potent level of healing resides, the Soul Truth.

Soul Truth

The third stage of healing is the most remarkable but also the most difficult to fathom. This is the level of the soul, and here we find the bottom line: the soul-level truth about ourselves. This is the truth of our perfection, our wholeness, and our wellness. Here is the opportunity to soar above the story—above causes and conditions—and know ourselves as we are in the Light of Truth. From this altitude, we can recognize all the dimensions and components of who we are as the elements of our infinite and loving soul. The essence of who we are now and who we have been through time reveals itself at this level. When we observe ourselves and our difficulties from this perspective, we may be startled to find ourselves in the midst of a powerful, heartfelt, loving experience.

Healing is under way as we move through these three levels within the Records: the story, the causes and conditions, and the Soul Truth. Herein lies the solution.

◆

Now that we are acquainted with the atmosphere of the Records, the possibilities for healing, and the progression of spiritual healing, it is time to clarify the nature of wounds, our access point to healing.

◆

CHAPTER TWO

Sacred Wounds

If you are reading this book, you are already aware of your woundedness. I know that this awareness is painful, but it truly means you are potentially in a wonderful place. Armed with this knowledge, you can become a conscious participant in your own experience of healing. You don't have to wait for someone else to save you, fix you, or relieve you of your distress—and in reality, no one else can do this for you anyway. Others can be supportive, but they can't go to those places within you where the hurt is all-consuming. Only you can go there on your own behalf.

Having set out on the quest of spiritual healing through the Akashic Records, you now begin the process of finding the way into the heart of your wounds. You will find your way back to your Innermost Self. Acceptance of your woundedness is the landing pad into healing.

What Do We Mean by Wounds?

So, when we speak of wounds, to what are we referring? Wounds are scars left behind by any kind of injury we have sustained—physical, emotional, or mental—that support negative ideas we have about ourselves, others, and life in general. They are caused by events that limit our ability to fully and freely express ourselves. All facets of our constitution are subject to life-altering injury that can thwart our development. It doesn't matter if the wound has come about through deliberate intent or by accident, overtly or covertly, consciously or unconsciously. It can be initiated by ourselves or by others. What makes an event a wound is that we use it against ourselves. We see it as evidence of our imperfection, and it then interferes with our ability to experience both our own goodness and the goodness of others.

Woundedness is universal. Everyone on the planet today is wounded, and everyone who has ever been alive was hurt, too. We have all been injured by others, and we have inflicted injury upon others, as well as ourselves—the whole of the human experience is a minefield of wounding. That this experience is universal is reflected in great literature and in every scriptural tradition; from our beginnings as humans we have shared stories about difficult, even horrific experiences. But while the experience is universal, it is also personal. When I have a broken heart, I am the one with a broken heart.

Wounds Become Issues

The injuries we suffer can result in terrible distortions in our perceptions, and this can limit our ability to experience the vitality of the life force. A devastating event can affect us in a way that makes it nearly impossible to engage effectively with our life, and this is tragic. What commonly occurs is that wounds morph into "issues," patterns we develop that interfere with our experience of the Innermost Self. For example, if a teacher makes a sarcastic remark about a young student's presentation, the child may decide then and there that he or she will never speak to a group again. If a parent walks out on the family unexpectedly, a child may respond by deciding not to get close to anyone else, thinking that this way he or she can escape rejection in the future. Our issues become excuses to avoid aspects of life we find difficult, crippling us physically, emotionally, and socially. This, of course, is the least desirable relationship we can have with our wounds.

From the Ordinary to the Sacred: A Matter of Perception

Because humans have suffered wounds for as long as we have been on earth, it makes sense to consider that there is a purpose—a spiritual purpose—for this wounding experience. There is a *sacred opportunity* within every wound: the chance to become aware of the Divine Reality through our own humanity. Difficult and often damaging human experiences form a crucible within which we encounter the Divine Presence. They offer us the opportunity to transform every aspect of our being, from our perceptions to the way we express ourselves in the world. They lead us to our Divine Destiny, which is to come to know our own essential goodness, the goodness of all others, and of life itself.

When does an ordinary wound become a sacred wound, one we can use to encounter the Divine? The event itself—the thing that hurts us—is not the determining factor. The difference is our *perception* of the occurrence. Using what has happened against ourselves, limiting our possibilities in life—this is ordinary. The wound becomes sacred when we shift our focus to the infinite possibility of our spiritual healing.

When we perceive our wounds as sacred, they indicate a path. As we walk this path, they become links to our own humanity, our connection to the humanity of others, and our point of contact with the Divine. They pierce our pride, enhance our awareness, and open the gates to new dimensions of aliveness.

Living a Paradox: Human and Divine

Our wounds serve to illustrate powerfully that we are human beings. If we lose a limb or suffer bodily trauma, we have tangible evidence that we are human. When we lose someone we love, there is awful, intense emotional pain, another reminder of our humanity. Even forgetfulness, indecision, and a confused mind demonstrate the inescapable truth that we are part of the human race. The human experience is one of limitation.

Awareness of our wounds can lead us to connection with other limited human beings who have been similarly injured. We can join forces, and the shared wounds become the doorway through which we pass together into healing. We can share solutions and grow beyond our difficulties, all the while enjoying the acceptance, understanding, and compassion of those who are walking a similar path.

The cost of admission to this fellowship of humanity is pride. Joining in community with others who have sustained a common injury and who are actively moving beyond the limitations it has imposed is a profound experience, one that requires humility. In order to correctly assess and accurately perceive ourselves, we must leave our pride at the door.

In a state of humility, we can accept the paradox of our identity. On one hand, we are limited human beings; on the other, we are unlimited, infinite, eternal. Put another way, we are unlimited beings in a limited situation. It is not helpful to hold our human constraints against ourselves or perceive them as flaws. Our limits are neither good nor bad.

From a humble stance, we can see that we are not the source of universal power. Instead, we are instruments of it, conduits for it. We are the space through which that power moves. Accepting our humanity and its limitations puts us in a position to receive this power—to be a human agent for Divine Life—and this can come as a huge relief. We no longer feel it is up to us to fix everything. We gain the freedom to let life unfold as it will and focus primarily on our own limited part of it. And the more we direct our attention to what we can genuinely impact, the more we experience satisfaction and success.

Developing these kinds of awareness and perceptions paves the way for changes in every area of our lives. "As within, so without" is a time-honored understanding: internal change is the forerunner to external change. Through this process of personal spiritual healing, we ascend (a topic I will discuss in greater detail in part 4), a state in which we continually rise above our current level of consciousness. Wherever we are now, there is a next level to which we can ascend—it's an infinite and eternal process resulting from inner attention and adjustments that facilitate an expanding awareness of oneness, conscious fusion with the Divine. We are now and have always been fused with the Divine: it is awareness of this fact that is the issue. Whenever we tap into the power of our Sacred Wounds, our consciousness of this eternal truth about ourselves expands—and we are healed and transformed.

Wounds as Gateways to Healing

So now you know the core truth of this system of healing through the Akashic Records. Our wounds—and the human limitations reflected in them—are the gateways to our spiritual healing. They are the core of our journey. Examining them as the sacred opportunities they truly are enables us to adjust our understanding to one that supports our spiritual development. We will investigate the true nature of our injuries, their purposefulness for developing consciousness, and the role they play as the threshold into greater dimensions of awareness. We will come to know our Sacred Wounds as a convergence point for transcendence, the zone through which we encounter the Divine Reality. And we will transmute each one from tragedy into exaltation, from a trapdoor into a gateway to greatness.

CHAPTER THREE

How to Read Your Akashic Records

Now we will begin our adventure in earnest by learning how to read our own Akashic Records. My objective here is to teach you everything you need to know about accessing the Records for the purpose of engaging in this three-stage journey of spiritual healing.

Let me be clear: we are not diving into a full course in Akashic Studies. Instead, we are covering a very specific aspect of activity within the Akasha. Our entryway into this dimension, from the sacred prayer tradition, is the Pathway Prayer Process to Access the Heart of the Records. We will examine the composition of the Prayer itself and the way the Records are organized. Before we are through, you will have a clear concept of what occurs when you are in the Records and know how to proceed in working with them.

If you are already initiated into the Pathway Prayer Process—through prior work with me or a Linda Howe– Certified Akashic Records Teacher, or even through my first book or audio set—you can use this chapter for review. Repetition is helpful; it will deepen your current level of comprehension and strengthen your skills.

If this is your very first exposure to the Akashic Records and your introduction to the Pathway Prayer Process to Access the Heart of the Records, let me say, "Welcome!"—you are embarking upon a profound journey of inner awareness. Let me also say, "Relax!" Please don't be concerned about what lies ahead. I will tell you everything you need to know to progress with this work. All you need to do is keep an open mind and take it one step at a time. This is not a race, so give yourself a chance to move along at a pace that is comfortable for you.

Over the years, I have taught many people how to do this with great results and I have observed, to a person, that those who have a sincere desire to learn how to access their Akashic Records are always able to do so.

I have told you *my* objective: to teach you what you need to know to work in your own Akashic Records and proceed with this personal healing project. This is a good time for you to consider your own objective. It is always empowering to take a moment and make a deliberate choice about what you hope to experience. Since this is your healing, you might want to begin with the goal of learning how to work in your Records well enough to take the next step in developing your consciousness, empowering yourself, and realizing healing. Clarity about the direction in which you are headed coupled with a conscious commitment to reach your objective helps keep you on track and propels you toward your desired end. Remain aware of your goals and your awareness will nurture you on the path.

A Closer Look at the Akashic Records

As we learned in chapter 1, the Records are the soul-level dimension of consciousness and contain the vibrational archive of every soul and its journey. Each soul's entry into the Records has two components, and these correspond to one another, forming a set. The first part of your Record is fixed—permanent and unchangeable. It is the essential blueprint of the soul. Another way to think of it is as your soul's fingerprint—your "soul print." It is unique, configured in a pattern that identifies your soul and no one else's. This is who you are as an expression of the Divine, and it is the part of yourself that you will become aware of as you journey though time, space, and human experience. When people say that the Akashic Records are permanent, this is what they are referring to: the fundamental pattern of the identity of the soul.

Traveling along with the essential soul print is the catalog of your lifetimes. As you progress through your incarnations, you awaken to your soul print, and as you experience this truth of yourself, you begin to live consciously soul-led lives. You become aware that your personal identity, your truest Self is Divine in nature, and your awareness expands to recognize this as true of all persons. In this part of the Records, there is a consistent theme but the details change: the specifics of each lifetime are variable and adjust as you grow and develop. Think of this second aspect of the Records as *The Chronicles of You Through Time.*

The primary concerns of the Records are:

- who you are,
- who you know yourself to be, and
- who you are becoming.

This is where themes come into play. An example of a theme is trusting your inner wisdom. It could take many lifetimes to learn how to do this. You may have multiple incarnations during which you ignore yourself, deny your inner promptings, reject your own insight, and listen to other people instead of yourself. You may have to live through this again and again before you recognize what you are doing and become impatient enough with it—no longer able to stand the futility of operating in this way—that you are willing to risk new behavior. Rewarded with good results from even a single experience of honoring your inner wisdom, you may try again. Seizing one opportunity at a time, you eventually move away from the old ways of doing things and act on your own inner guidance.

In some lifetimes, you may do this impulsively, hastily acting on everything that goes through your mind. During other incarnations, you may misinterpret or misunderstand what you are hearing when you listen to your inner voice through trial and error. At still other times, you may feel foolish for following your hunches, but this, too, is part of the learning process. You are discovering which inner voices deserve attention, how to listen to yourself, and how to decipher the guidance you are receiving. Considering how many dimensions there are to this, it may take a few lifetimes to learn how to do this well.

The length of time it takes for this evolution to progress is a secondary matter. In the grand scheme of the universe, which is infinite, it doesn't really matter if it takes ten lifetimes or nine hundred. It doesn't matter if you awaken to the truth of your being while living as a male or a female, on a tropical island or on a fishing boat in the Bering Sea. While these details may be interesting, they are not the point of the story; the point is learning the lesson and applying it in a way that is supportive.

Themes such as this are constant, even though the details change. What is absolutely fixed is that at some point in time and space on the Earth plane, you will come into an honorable relationship with your own inner knowing. This is an essential part of your destiny as a soul. How, when, and where this occurs is flexible and is determined by your free will.

Choice and our relationship with the act of choosing itself are key to human experience, and conscious choosing is an evolutionary step we all attain somewhere along the way as our soul journeys. Making conscious choices establishes our awareness of, and maintains our alignment with, the essential Divine Truth—it supports our awakening. This is how the human experience of a soul's travel through space and time unfolds. The Akashic Records hold the archives of all our journeys toward this awakening over the great span of time.

As I mentioned in chapter 1, the Akashic Records are made up of the Akasha. *Akasha* is a Sanskrit word meaning "primary substance, that out of which all things are formed."* This substance is a vibrational record that is invisible to the human eye but discernible to the subtle senses, which are heightened when we open the Records. The Akasha is so sensitive that all thoughts and everything that happens are registered within it. While it holds all that has ever been, it also reflects our current state of consciousness. Past, present, and future thoughts and experiences are all held within the Records, and they are available to us whenever they might be useful.

Perhaps now you see why I have described the Akashic Records as an infinite spiritual resource; they contain an abundance of information we can put to use for personal healing. When we move into this realm of vibrational consciousness, we become more receptive than usual, and in this state we can explore. We can make the acquaintance of our Innermost Self and learn who we have been in this lifetime and in other lives. Our future possibilities—both immediate and long-range— are surprisingly accessible. Make no mistake: the Records are not a funhouse full of stories for our entertainment. Instead they are a rich treasury of information steeped in a culture of wisdom and compassion: they are available to support us in our evolution. When we approach the Records with respect for their sacred nature and a sincere heart, everything we need in order to take the next step in our journey becomes available.

Interestingly, despite the fact that the future is contained within them, the Records are not the best tool for divining

---

*From *The Aquarian Gospel of Jesus the Christ* by Levi H. Dowling, Camarillo, CA: DeVorss Publications, p.10.

the future. This is because they concern themselves with the "who" and the "why" rather than the "what" and "when" of life. For the very same reason—the emphasis on who and why—the Akashic Records offer remarkable support for personal empowerment and awareness. They form a safe space within which we can learn the truth of who we are, discover why life is unfolding as it is, let go of what does not work, and explore more supportive options.

The Soul's Perspective

The Records serve as an internal pathway of Light through which we can safely travel into our own experience of the Divine Reality—however we may understand that concept. As a soul-level dimension of consciousness, the Records occupy an altitude from which we can perceive ourselves and others in the Light of the Akasha. When we open the Records, we have an opportunity to perceive everything from the perspective of the soul. We glimpse the soul-level truth of ourselves and can more easily recognize the choices, experiences, people, activities, and other elements of life that will support our living in conscious alignment with who we are. From this perspective, actualizing our Divine potential becomes a real possibility.

The Records at This Time in History

This is a particularly exciting time in history for the Akashic Records. Until the end of the twentieth century, this resource was the exclusive domain of mystics, scholars, and saints— with a few exceptions. Now we are waking up to greater truth, individually and collectively, and the Records have become available as a spiritual resource for us all.

An important development has made way for the Records to be present for all of us: organized religions have failed to meet the needs of many people—and this remains a growing trend. Historically, traditional religions have been essential for socialization, for providing a place to belong, and for establishing structure—all critical components of harmonious living in communities. For those looking for an experience of the Divine Reality, traditional religions may not be much help. They comprise an *external* structure through which many of us have hoped to encounter Divine Life. That they have largely failed isn't much of a surprise, for the Divine is an internal experience. In contrast to religions, the Akashic Records form an interior Bridge of Light that facilitates our journey to the level of the Divine. I have come to understand that the Records are now available to us in response to a tremendous cry welling up from humanity, seeking this experience. This is truly our birthright; we are entitled to know our own soul and to have a more conscious relationship with the Divine.

There is also a shift in how the Records are being used. Edgar Cayce (1877–1945), known as the "sleeping prophet," was the first to popularize the Akashic Records as a resource for healing. He performed his work within the Records while unconscious; still, the transmissions he received were remarkably helpful during his time and continue to be so to this day. Over the past half century, the Records have been used consciously as a spiritual resource for personal empowerment and consciousness development.

So you find yourself coming to the Records at a wonderful time, when they are yours to explore. You don't have to be clairvoyant or religious, a scholar or a saint. Trust me, if sainthood were a requirement, I would be denied access! The Akashic Records let me in whenever I am moved to open them, and they will let you in, too.

Guidelines for Working in the Records

As you might have imagined, there are guidelines for working in the Records that will ensure a positive experience. Let me be clear: the purpose of these guidelines is to support you in your Akashic Records' practice. They are not intended to cramp your style or limit your exploration in any way. It is simply true that if you follow these recommendations, you will do better work in the Records than if you ignore them. Also, if you adhere to them it will be easier for you to trust the results you get. Working in the Records is a discipline—a spiritual discipline—and as with any other kind of discipline, following certain protocols leads to greater success. Having taught thousands of people how to do this, I have noticed that those who respect the guidelines give better readings than those who do not: the greater the adherence, the deeper they can go.

Guideline 1: *Do not consume drugs or alcohol within twenty-four hours of opening the Records.*

The energy of the Akashic Records is very quick—think of the speed of light. These recreational substances weaken the boundary of your energy field, making it more difficult for you to hold or manage this highly accelerated Light and maintain yourself in its presence. If you have enjoyed recreational drugs or alcohol within twenty-four hours of opening the Records, you will not have the crisp edge you need. I am not saying you should not use recreational drugs or alcohol; that is your choice. Just wait at least twenty-four hours before you open the Records. You will get much more productive results.

Guideline 2: *Use your current legal name when opening the Records.*

This means your legal name today, if it is not the same as your birth name. Your legal name is the one that appears on your taxes and other documents of that nature. The issue here is vibration: your name has a vibrational identity. When your name is made legal, it is established on the earth plane as your commitment to the probabilities and possibilities of that identity. And yes, when you change your name legally, you actually change your probabilities. If you don't like your name, consider changing it. Until then, though, use the legal name that is yours today for best results.

Guideline 3: *Be responsible for your time in the Records.*

The first area of responsibility involves taking note of how much time you intend to spend with your Records open at any given opportunity. Being responsible in this way will support you in cultivating depth and richness in your practice. When you first start working in them, it is important to give yourself a chance to acclimate to the energy. So in the beginning, it is a good idea to keep the Records open for at least ten to fifteen minutes at a time. Working in the Records is a lot like building muscle. You always possess the "muscle" of the Records, but you are just beginning to learn to use it. Take the time to develop it, slowly and well. Make note of how long you plan to stay in the Records, and when the time has elapsed, close them. Remember that you can always go back at a later time. Clear boundaries support the flow of great power in spiritual practices, as well as in everyday life; use them to gain strength.

When you first start working in the energy field of the Records, you may not be able to focus for more than fifteen or twenty minutes. That is absolutely appropriate. There is no need to keep them open for an hour if you cannot stay steady in the Light of Akasha for that long. It is always better doing thirty potent minutes than sixty sloppy ones. Pay attention to how you are feeling and honor your own pace.

Another area where it is wise to be responsible is to devote your time in the Records solely to them. It is usually not helpful to multitask or to attempt to use the Records to augment some other activity, particularly at first. There is no evidence, for example, that opening the Records before bed will result in more productive dreams. In fact, the opposite is true, because your attention is divided. It is best to be single-minded in focus when dealing with altered states of consciousness. People sometimes open the Records and then go to their jobs, hoping to gain some insight into what's going on there. This, too, detracts from both experiences.

Absolutely do not drive with open Records—traffic and the meditative state of the Records are a bad combination.

This guideline of responsibility addresses drawbacks including the dangers of multitasking. However, after you have practiced being in your Akashic Records for some time, if you find you would like to try experimenting by combining the Records work with some other spiritual activities, by all means go ahead. Some people successfully do feng shui sessions while in the Records, for example, or examine their astrological chart. Just be sure you are familiar with what the Records are and how they work within you first. Once you have a clear sense of their energy—for most people this is after at least thirty days—you can proceed with some exploration.

Guideline 4: *Ground yourself after each reading.*

This simple suggestion can make a world of difference. Opening and closing the Records involves moving from one state of consciousness to another. You are shifting from a regular, everyday state of awareness to a highly sensitized state and then back to your normal one. You can wind up feeling a bit spacey or disoriented from this transitioning back and forth. This is not a problem per se, but if you get behind the wheel of your car in this woozy condition, you could cause some real trouble. After closing the Records, take a moment to perform some action that is grounding. Have a drink of water, step outside for some fresh air, water the plants, or touch your toes: any activity that reminds you of the fact that you do indeed have a body, are a normal person living a regular life, and are a resident of planet Earth will do the trick.

Guideline 5: *When combining work in the Akashic Records with any other spiritual practice, always honor both.*

Conversely, if the guidelines and procedures for a particular system you use conflict with the guidelines for using the Records, do not use them at the same time. For example, if another spiritual practice involves ingesting a hallucinogenic substance, do not work in the Records while you are under its influence. One path at a time is sufficient in itself, and it will not be helpful to either practice if both cannot be honored.

The Sacred Prayer Tradition and the Pathway Prayer Process

People access the Records in a variety of ways—through hypnosis, reiki, and any number of spiritual disciplines. An individual is attracted to the method that suits him or her—it's a matter of a vibrational match, a way to gain access that best fits the individual soul print and can be easily recognized. I have found the pathway I offer here to be exceptionally effective for many people, and the fact that you have arrived at this chapter offers a clue that it has great possibilities for you, too.

With this means of access, we are working within the Sacred Prayer tradition. In this tradition, we use a prayer that is composed of specific words configured in stanzas that have a certain rhythm. As you say this prayer, two processes occur simultaneously.

First, we move from one state of consciousness into another, from our regular level of awareness into a receptive, sensitized state of heightened perception. We maintain full consciousness, but we are able to recognize and register subtleties in the atmosphere that we have not previously discerned. When we work in the Records, the shift in our consciousness must be sufficient to register the impressions of the Akasha.

The second process that occurs from using the Prayer is that you are transformed at the level of your own heart. There is a correspondence between the Heart of the Akashic Records and your personal heart; through the Prayer, they move into alignment, into a relationship of reciprocal support. In this developing relationship, the heart begins to take the lead within your consciousness and the mind shifts into the service of your heart. This is happening within mass consciousness now. We have lived a long time in the service of our minds, but at present, we are in a time of transformation—our human faculties are reorganizing to serve the wisdom and goodness of our hearts. Consider the possibility that you have been drawn to this work by your soul's prompting because you are a person with a powerful heart who is ready to live your life in the service of love.

The Sacred Prayer you will use is the Pathway Prayer Process to Access the Heart of the Akashic Records. This Prayer came to me in 2001 after I had been working in the Records for seven years—developing a very rich and meaningful relationship with the Records—and teaching for five years. The great blessing of this Prayer is that it enabled me, and has since enabled countless others, to move into the very Heart of the Akasha and to mine this realm at its most energy-rich location. It also provides the energetic support to integrate the heart, mind, and will so you can operate in the Records as a fully synthesized being.

How to Use the Pathway Prayer Process

Now we have come to the Prayer you will use to open the Records: The Pathway Prayer Process to Access the Heart of the Akashic Records. You will first examine how it is composed and then learn how to use it to gain entry into the Records. There are two main parts: the Opening Prayer and the Closing Prayer. The Opening Prayer has three stanzas with lines numbered one through eleven. The lines of the Closing Prayer are not numbered. Both sections of this prayer are required to formally open and close the Records. The Opening Prayer will move you into the soul-level dimension of the Akasha. Using the Closing Prayer returns you to your original state of consciousness.

To open your Akashic Records, follow these three steps:

1. Say lines 1 through 10 of the Opening Prayer aloud, inserting "myself" or "me" as appropriate where you find these words in italics in lines 8 through 10.

2. Repeat lines 8 through 10 silently two more times, inserting your current legal name where the italics appear.

3. Announce the opening of the Records by saying line 11 aloud.

Opening Prayer

1. And so we do acknowledge the Forces of Light,
2. Asking for guidance, direction, and courage to know the Truth
3. As it is revealed for our highest good and the highest good of
4. Everyone connected to us.
5. Oh Holy Spirit of God
6. Protect me from all forms of self-centeredness
7. And direct my attention to the work at hand.
8. Help me to know (*myself*) in the Light of the Akashic Records,
9. To see (*myself*) through the eyes of the Lords of the Records,
10. And enable me to share the wisdom and compassion that the Masters, Teachers, and Loved Ones of (*me*) have for (*me*).
11. The Records are now open.

That is the process for opening your Akashic Records. When it is time to close them, read the Closing Prayer aloud once:

Closing Prayer

I would like to thank the Masters, Teachers, and Loved Ones for their love and compassion.

I would like to thank the Lords of the Akashic Records for their point of view.

And I would like to thank the Holy Spirit of Light for all knowledge and healing.

The Records are now closed. Amen.
The Records are now closed. Amen.
The Records are now closed. Amen.

It is surprisingly simple, isn't it? Try it a few times to see how it works. Remember that you are a beginner now, and you may find yourself experiencing some hesitation. This is perfectly natural—just let yourself play with it. Don't feel pressured to achieve sudden enlightenment or get to the root of a long-standing life issue. Right now you are just getting used to the coming and going, the flow, the atmosphere, and your sense of it all. And that is enough at this stage. After you have practiced a few times, move on to the next section to learn how the Records are organized. This information will make it easier for you to trust the process.

How the Akashic Records Are Organized

When we work in the Records, we engage with energy first, information second. The energies of the Akasha are governed by the three Absolutes of the Akasha described earlier in this book: "Judge Not," "Fear Not," "Resist Not." These governing principles provide an atmosphere of kindness and respect within which we can do our soul searching and healing. Knowing these as the energetic underpinnings of the Records, we can fully expect to be well treated; there is no teasing, ridicule, or torment. If we happen to encounter attitudes of this sort, we can be absolutely certain that we are *not* in the Akashic Records. The three Absolutes help us know beyond a doubt when we are within the realm and when we are not. If we are not, we always have another opportunity to say the Prayer and gain entry.

The Energetic Entities of the Akashic Records

Now that we are acquainted with the Records and know how to access them, it's time to meet the energetic beings residing there, all of whom are called upon in the Pathway Prayer Process. There are four "departments" of the Records, and they are managed by four different groups of energetic entities, identified by their responsibilities and characteristics. This is not a world of spirit guides, angels, or channeled entities—those are wonderful, but this is different. In those worlds, we can recognize our unseen helpers by their personalities. In the Records, our unseen helpers are known by their service. We humans are easily fascinated and distracted by glamorous personalities, and this can sometimes take our attention away from the central focus of our inner work, which is to mature as people, develop our faculties, and become our best human selves. This is why within the Records, we work with energies instead of personalities. Ultimately, the personality is the vehicle for the ego, and the spiritual quest is about gaining freedom from the demands of the ego, not inflating its allure.

Each group of beings managing the Records stays within its own arena, but all the beings work together in concert to maintain the flow of energy and information from the Records to us, the requesters. One group is focused on the Records themselves and the other three are involved with our journey. Let's take a look at who they are, what they do, and what we can expect from them.

The Lords of the Akashic Records

This group is entrusted with the well-being of the Records themselves—this is their exclusive focus. They maintain the Records' integrity and sanctity so they do not become corrupted or compromised in any way. We never see the Lords of the Records; they do not show us their faces. They are not embodied and have never been, so do not be offended that you will not meet them. This is exactly as it should be.

The Lords of the Records interact with the Masters, the first in the group of three whose focus is on us and our growth. The Lords assist the Masters in "downloading" the energy and information we require at any given time.

The Masters

The Masters remain in relationship with an individual soul from the point of the soul's inception and throughout time. Though the Masters are not embodied either, one way to think of the relationship here is that while the Lords of the Records face the Records themselves with their backs to us, the Masters stand back to back with the Lords, facing us. They work very closely with the Lords to transmit whatever guidance, wisdom, or insight we may need at any given time to continue our growth and evolution. Your Masters determine who your Teachers are, the sequence of the expansion of your awareness, and who your Loved Ones will be during each lifetime.

Basically, your Masters are in charge of your journey through time and space.

The Teachers

Many spiritual systems use the term "teacher," so let's be clear about what "Teacher" means in the realm of Akasha. Within this system, Teachers may or may not have been embodied at one time, but currently they are not. Their role is lesson specific, not soul specific. Each Teacher is responsible for developing a specific understanding within an individual—the Teacher's special area of expertise—and once this is achieved, the Teacher will go on to the next person who is ready to comprehend the idea. If you are dealing with healing and self-doubt in this lifetime, then you will have a Teacher who will help you learn how to go beyond that state and move into self-trust. As we learned in our discussion of themes, it does not matter if this takes five lifetimes or five hundred; the Teacher whose specialty is mastery of self-trust will be with you until you, too, become a master of it. At that point, your Masters will determine what is the next best step in your growth and will send the appropriate Teacher to enable your success.

The Loved Ones

Loved Ones are people you have known in this lifetime—the lifetime you currently occupy—who are now deceased and are assisting from the other side. You may or may not have a strong personal attachment to these individuals. One of your Loved Ones could be your favorite aunt. Just as likely, though, one might be a childhood schoolteacher who seemed to have a good sense of you or even one who may have played the role of devil's advocate, challenging you to achieve your potential. The Loved Ones are committed to developing your awareness as a soul and to encouraging you from a soul perspective. Don't expect the Loved Ones to be available for interaction; while we may invite them to chat, they will likely decline. They do not do "readings," such as those that take place in mediumistic practices. Our Loved Ones are simply available to support our development. We can sense their presence, which can be comforting, motivating, or reflective of another quality then needed. The specific qualities we receive are those they embodied during their lives and those we enjoyed in our relationships with them.

As a matter of course, you will not see the Loved Ones or know their names. You will not have personal relationships with them, as that could actually detract from your own expanding awareness and growth. It is more important to them that you engage the energy of the Records, apply the insights, guidance, and wisdom you find there, and fully mine this treasury of spiritual riches.

How the Records Reveal Themselves: What You Can Expect

It is welcome news to most of us that we do not have to be psychic to engage in the Akashic Records work. This is because the Records are a soul-level resource, and each of us has a soul—or more accurately, *is* a soul. Consequently, it is perfectly natural and well within our abilities to explore the Akasha.

We receive the energy and information of the Records in a variety of ways, ranging from hearing to seeing to a sense of knowing. Eighty-five percent of the people who work in the Records receive information through their sense of knowing. This means that only fifteen percent actually encounter an inner vision or hear a voice. You can reasonably expect to experience the wisdom of the Records as a hunch or as an "It sure seems like" realization. In this realm, those are perfectly valid starting places—remember, this can be subtle work. "Take what you get" is a good suggestion to help you receive from the Records at first. What's important is that you find out for yourself how energy and guidance come to you, and this will require some experimentation. Wherever you begin, your starting place will be perfect for you, and you can grow from there.

The Records are dynamic and interactive. This is not a passive practice: you do not open the Records and get bombarded with energy and information. At the same time, the Records are vast—infinite, actually—which can be overwhelming. To avoid feeling overwhelmed—and its counterpart, paralysis—we use a very helpful strategy: we ask questions. Questions are terrific, especially open-ended questions. A question beginning with "Why" is the most powerful type you can ask, as "why" deals with the forces that drive events. Remember, the primary concern of the Records is who we are becoming through our human journey, and so the "why" question can be illuminating. That which is occurring behind the scenes to cause what actually appears in our lives is "where the action is" in the Records.

As touched on previously, "when" is not the most effective question to ask, as time in the Records is simply not as significant as it is to us here on the Earth plane. "When" in the Records is a chronology, a sequence of events. If you want to know when you are going to meet your soul mate from the point of view of the Records, you will probably meet him or her after you forgive your brother and clean your basement and help the old lady next door by shoveling her snow. Exact dates and times are not the focus of the Records.

Yes/no questions are far less productive than open-ended ones. "Should" is not helpful because there are no "shoulds" in the Records. When you ask, "What should I do?" the Records normally suggest that you "should" do what makes you happy or gives you peace, or you "should" make your own decisions.

It is beneficial to ask questions that help you explore your issues, shed light on your concerns, and help you gain clarity and insight into whatever difficulties are presenting themselves. In the final analysis, we must make our own choices, and the Records will support us as we do so. The Records are not in the business of depriving us of opportunities to evaluate our options, make our selections, and live with the consequences of our choices. And because of this, the Records function as a resource for our personal empowerment. Rather than deciding for us, they lend wisdom, guidance, and energetic support as we live our lives. The result is growth, expanded awareness, and healing.

How to Proceed from Here

This has been the express-lane course in how to read your Akashic Records. You now have enough information to use them for your personal healing adventure. At the same time, you are still a beginner, and I want you to be realistic about that fact—it is a perfectly fine place to be right now. Practice and more practice is the key to gaining experience, and experience is the ticket to improvement. Please feel free to open your Records as much as you like; there is no such thing as working in them too much. If you are overdoing it, you will find yourself getting bored or receiving the same answers again and again. In this way, the Akashic Records are a self-correcting path.

For best results in your journey of spiritual healing, keep your attention on questions for reflection, those I provide for you here, and your own questions that will arise as you become comfortable with this practice. Focus on the answers. Do not over-concern yourself with whether or not your guidance comes from the Records. Move forward one step at a time. The Pathway Prayer says, "Direct my attention to the work at hand," and this phrase will shepherd you safely into the Heart of the Akasha.

As I mentioned earlier, if you would like more detailed instruction on how to read the Akashic Records, you can turn to my book of the same name. I have also recorded a six-CD learning set, also titled *How to Read the Akashic Records*. Both are excellent helpmates to you on your journey.

I will leave you with a final thought before we dive into the crux of this book. If you have doubts, if you are saying to yourself, "I just don't know about this Pathway Prayer Process," that is fine. Feel free to engage in this spiritual healing practice using any method that suits you. The work itself is universal. I invite you to try the Pathway Prayer first, though, because it was the key that unlocked this healing system for me. It may just be the ideal gateway for the unique three-stage healing system you are about to encounter.

Our Sacred Wounds as Points of Power in Our Relationship with Ourselves

PART TWO

Introduction

Now that you have an overview of the Akashic Records, know how to access them, and have learned some of what you can expect to find there, you are prepared to enter the first phase of healing: exploring your Sacred Wounds as a point of power in your relationship with your Innermost Self. Here you will examine your own injuries, the impact they have had on you, and how they have governed you and influenced the way you have structured your self-expression. It is time to discover how the inner cries for help embedded in your wounds provide an invitation to a deeper, more intimate, and more powerful relationship with the richest, most precious part of yourself.

Spiritual expansion is a forerunner to effective emotional healing. When we have a strong sense of trust in the innate goodness of life, it becomes easier to let go of limiting patterns, old pain, and outdated ideas. When we feel safe, we can "let go" into something greater or better, not into some murky unknown. So, as a way to support and accelerate your journey, I invite you to frequently entertain ideas of all that is good in life, as well as of life's trustworthy nature. This can be as simple as reminding yourself that the sun always rises in the east, gravity never fails, and the seasons follow a predictable path. Activating your awareness of the harmony and order in life can be a reassuring and balancing force as you venture into some of the messier areas of your inner realms.

It is good to practice this whenever you find yourself at an emotional impasse, such as being unable to forgive for fear of sanctioning injustice, or holding on to hardened feelings to keep from exposing yourself to further pain. This is exactly the time to try to enlarge your spiritual life and awareness of the spiritual nature of life itself. Doing so expands the energetic safety net, so you can move through the healing process more quickly and effectively.

To get yourself unstuck ask, "How can I expand my awareness of spiritual truth?" One of the great spiritual laws is "Seek and you shall find." Begin seeking the spiritual truth of the trustworthy nature of life. Open the Records and ask to be able to recognize the ways in which the world *is* a safe place: you have supportive friends, or even though you've been through some rough times, you have always managed to stand on your own two feet in the end. Ask to see the fundamental order of life on this planet. As you ask, you will begin to see more clearly, and as you see and gather evidence that it is safe to trust, you will relax further into the energetic safety net. It will become easier than ever to let go of old ways and grow into your new possibilities.

At this point in our process—as we begin the first phase of this grand adventure—I want to make clear that the Innermost Self is a facet of the soul. To refresh, the soul is that part of us that knows itself to be Divine in nature. The Innermost Self is the aspect of the soul that recognizes the sacred nature of being and acts as gatekeeper—a position with significant responsibilities and privileges. The Innermost Self is a dimension of being that protects our richest resources: such things as our creativity and our capacity for intimacy. The Innermost Self has the extraordinary privilege of determining how we will harness and direct the vital life-force energy.

A Four-Step Progression for Transformation

We are going to learn to transform our relationship to our wounds for the purpose of consciously connecting with ourselves. This involves a four-step progression: Awareness of Self, Self-Acceptance, Appropriate Action, and Choice. While these qualities are all related—and once activated, work as a unit—they are also distinct. As you contemplate the power inherent in each, you may find that one is of greater concern to you than another. This is valuable information. Pay attention to your responses; they will help inform and direct your healing work.

Awareness of Self

The first step is Awareness of Self. At this level, we wake up to the fact that we are ourselves. We become aware that deep at the center of our being is a part of us that has always been there: our Innermost Self has paid attention to us our entire life. This is the part of you that is you, that has always been you, and will always be you. It was with you on the first day of class at school, on the playground, and as you hung out with your friends as a teenager. It has been listening to your stories and arguments and commentary about yourself and life, listening to what you have to say about everything and how you are navigating this incarnation. When we speak of Awareness of Self in the context of healing and strengthening our relationship with ourselves, consciousness of this constant companion is what we mean.

Self-Acceptance

Next is Self-Acceptance. Truly accepting who you are—and who you are not—is a profound spiritual action that yields incredible results. The practice begins with the spiritual discipline of extending unconditional love to yourself. This involves offering yourself unlimited understanding and compassion—no matter what you do or don't do, no matter how you respond under any and all conditions. Unconditional love is a great *idea,* but it is particularly remarkable as a *spiritual practice.* As an ongoing exercise, it facilitates your healing, sometimes beyond your wildest dreams.

Appropriate Action

Appropriate Action is the third step in our four-step progression toward personal transformation. This is the level at which you address the business of taking action on your own behalf. In all spiritual work, there are both inner and outer aspects: Self-Acceptance is an inner dimension and Appropriate Action is an outer one. Action is a critical piece because we are alive on this Earth—our spiritual journey is more than a theory. It is something we live, something we do. In this plane of existence—the realm of incarnation, of spirit becoming form—one of our primary challenges is to recognize that the material is spiritual and the spiritual is material. We achieve this understanding through action.

Choice

The fourth step is Choice. From a spiritual perspective, you are your soul's first choice. Out of all the other possibilities in the universe, your soul picked you. For some, this is a radical concept with life-changing potential. It is the overarching basis for our healing. The other three steps bring the structure of your internal reality into the present so you can acclimate to this wonderful reality. You discover that as you choose to be with yourself, to love yourself unconditionally, and to act on your own behalf, you naturally move into a state of conscious alignment and fusion with yourself. And then the Innermost Self opens the gate, and the unique treasury of *life as you* is revealed. The Innermost Self releases power, creativity, insight, love, and joy—all the goodness that is within you—as it finds expression through you.

◆

Knowing the possibilities awaiting you, let's move on to the specific practices that we will employ to heal our relationships, beginning with our relationship to our Self.

CHAPTER FOUR

Awareness of Self

In this chapter we will examine Awareness of Self—the Self described earlier who has always been our companion, the Innermost Self. In developing self-awareness, it is necessary to explore a key concept in spiritual healing: self-abandonment. Becoming aware of the ways in which we forsake ourselves is an essential step in healing our relationship with ourselves.

It is curious that awareness of the Innermost Self would even be an issue. We are with ourselves all the time: there is no holiday, nor should there be. Yet for many of us, awareness of the Innermost Self dims as we make our human trek across the planet. What could possibly cause such a fading of consciousness, and what are the consequences of it?

Choices that override the impulses of the Innermost Self, whether dismissive or antagonistic, result in significantly less awareness of its very existence. The consequence is a state of deprivation: we have denied ourselves a sacred relationship, our birthright, our entitlement, to a conscious connection with our soul. We have a blessed opportunity, through this lifetime, to get to know who we are; to cultivate our gifts, talents, and abilities; and to enjoy ourselves. When instead we deny ourselves, push ourselves away, or try to make ourselves something other than who we are, we create a situation of self-abandonment and self-rejection. It is impossible to cultivate a relationship of self-awareness while simultaneously denying or diminishing ourselves. It's like trying to be awake and asleep at the same instant—human beings can only occupy one state of awareness at a time.

Becoming Aware of Self-Abandonment

None of us, it seems, would deliberately reject our very selves unless it somehow appeared to be a good idea in the moment. We always seek our own good, what is best as we journey through life. The question then becomes, what could convince us that self-abandonment is a viable option?

Self-abandonment is the king of the Sacred Wounds hall of fame, so let's take this opportunity to become more conscious of it. Let's examine what it is, how it's created, and what to do about this debilitating condition.

The Akashic Records reveal that each time a soul enters a new life, the current consciousness determines the choice of a family of origin. A particular birth family is chosen because it reflects our present perception of self, others, and the whole of life. Like it or not, all these family members are in sync—only people who share vibrations and level of consciousness can be together. This is one of the fundamental laws of life. You have probably heard the sayings "Water seeks its own level" and "Birds of a feather flock together." It cannot be otherwise.

The partner to this truth is another law of life: the law of ongoing growth and expansion. While people can only be in arenas of matching vibration, expansion, evolution, and change are always occurring. This means we are always on the move from one aspect of being to another—sometimes quickly, sometimes slowly, but always moving, even when it appears otherwise. In fact, a static state is impossible: we are made up of living atoms that continuously vibrate. Even if this activity is not discernible to the human eye, it is nonetheless under way. We may stay with the people we have chosen, or we may leave. Whatever is best for the evolution of consciousness is what comes to pass. There is always opportunity to grow beyond where we are at any given moment, even if we are in a most fabulous place. What lies beyond fabulous? Even more splendid! This is an infinite universe filled with endless opportunities.

And so we encounter another human paradox. On the one hand, we chose our family of origin as a perfect reflection of our current level of consciousness; on the other, we are with them for our growth and evolution, so we may stay or go as our destinies dictate. We come into this life with a certain set of ideas, assumptions, and beliefs. The chosen situation provides the support necessary to mirror our present consciousness, to bring us face to face with our inner truths made manifest. Beliefs and cherished personal truths form our Earthly reality. Recognizing and taking responsibility for our reality positions us for change.

During the first seven years of life, a child experiences herself as one and the same as her parent or primary caregiver. You selected your caregivers to reinforce your beliefs during these years, and as a result, energetically, your beliefs hardened like sun-baked clay. They then become the filter through which you interpret the rest of your life. Until and unless there is some kind of awakening, this is the lens through which you will continue to view life. You will develop a very specific point of view, and as long as you have it, that is how everything will appear to you—no matter the other realities present. This serves to erect an obvious and unavoidable physical representation of your belief structure, which, when identified, can be released.

During those first seven years, if the consciousness that is the child is generally pleased with herself, she will choose parents who are pleased with her. If the child is unhappy with who she is, she will pick parents who will reflect that perception back to her. It *appears* that the parent is the determining factor in the child's self-perception, but it is actually the other way around. The parental influence is very powerful, though, and will "lock in" the beliefs the child holds.

Of course, no one is 100 percent one way or another. Nobody is always pleased or always unhappy. We are all a blend, with some aspects that are wonderful and some not so much—this is the nature of our soul's progression. If we are pleased with who we are 51 percent of the time, our parents will reflect that back to us.

Causes of Self-Abandonment

If a child experiences a needy moment, reaches out to a parent, and finds the parent unavailable, there is a jolt to his system, and the child interprets this lack of availability as rejection. It is important to recognize that there is no energetic distinction between real unmet needs and rejection—"Get away from me. You make me sick. I hate you!"—and temporary lack of availability: "I'm bathing your brother, and I need to make sure he stays safe—I can't be there for you now." Both kinds of "rejection" equally affect the Light Grid that holds our identity in place, and the pattern for self-rejection and self-abandonment is set.

Another kind of interaction that results in a painful pattern of self-abandonment—of pushing love away, including love of self—is one in which there are conflicting messages concerning punishment and love: "I'm punishing you (yelling at you, hitting you) because I love you!" This is completely confusing, and the child will learn to interpret punishment, anger, and judgment as love. As this experience is repeated and hardens in the Light Grid, the child will begin to seek rejection and abuse, not because this is what he truly wants, but because pain felt has become confused with the love needed.

Self-abandonment can even arise from compassion. If a parent suffers pain, whether physical or emotional, the child may leave herself behind and extend her love and support to her parent. This is the most natural of all human responses, and it is loving in its original intent. A problem arises when the child does not see the presence of Light in her parent, because the parent does not see it either.

Once such ideas are set in place—that one is being rejected, whether true or not; it is good to be rejected because it means one is loved; that abandoning oneself to care for another is a good thing—our relationship with ourselves is fraught with pain. We are being guided by very confusing ideas about connection and intimacy and have little potential for a satisfactory relationship to our Innermost Self. Some of the examples I have just described may seem extreme—and they are—but know that there is a continuum of experiences. Most of us become wounded with a little bit of this and a dash of that. Any combination of these kinds of parent-child dynamics can be a prescription for misery.

When these beliefs become set as the internal structure through which we interpret our life experiences, our personal Light Grid responds and adapts to reflect them.

To reinforce some of the principles we have discussed so far, we have this progression: you enter into this life with a very specific level of consciousness, choosing people and circumstances that will help you see what you consider to be the truth. Then your Light Grid, or pattern, becomes deeply etched by painful experiences of rejection and confusion. But here comes the good news: the Akashic Records hold the blueprint, your soul print, and the pattern of your Light Grid. As you examine yourself in the kindness and safety of the Records, *the grid changes*—quickly and easily. You can shift the energies in your grid yourself, and as you pull the plug on old patterns, you can choose to establish new ones. Amazing!

Until you do so, however, feelings such as self-abandonment, self-rejection, and confusion about love may dominate your grid and filter your beliefs, and plenty of difficulties will result. You can meet people who genuinely love and appreciate you and sincerely extend themselves to you in love, but from an energetic perspective, you have no "receptor sites" for their nurturing, loving energy. It's simply impossible for you to receive their love, to allow their goodwill to touch your heart. Sadly, despite your good intentions, your desires, and even your deliberate strategizing to bring more love into your life, you may be unable to receive or hold their loving energy.

Directing Attention Within

Many of us who have been on a spiritual path for some time have spent decades working on our issues with other people, addressing the destructive effects of our painful interactions with others and the harm done to our healthy development. Yes, we may have glimpses of relief from time to time, but they do not last. This is because our efforts have missed their proper target—they have been sincere, but misguided. We have aimed toward the space between us and the other when the root of the difficulty—and the power for transformation—lies within us.

Now, more than ever before, we are each responsible for the condition of our own Light Grid. Our job as awakening beings is to adjust our own patterns. Our authority lies within ourselves, and as we resolve our inner misperceptions, our outer lives move into harmony. It is futile to wait for another to accept us first, thinking we will then follow suit: we will not. It is our responsibility to establish ourselves as "self-acceptors." One of the laws of the universe is that "no one can give you what you cannot give yourself." Put another way, people can only give to you to the limit of what you are willing to offer yourself. If you have a blend of some of the difficulties I have described, as most of us do—a dose of self-rejection, a dash of self-abandonment—other people, whether they mean to or not, will reflect this swirl of ideas back to you through your perception of their actions. But when you clear up your own false mythologies, you will find others treating you with increasing respect and understanding.

Our goal in healing is to arrive at a place in our relationship with ourselves where we are free from any need to leave ourselves, where we can stay with ourselves no matter what, and where we honor ourselves with kindness and dignity. Once we have this newly configured Light Grid—once our behavior toward ourselves has become honorable—others cannot help but treat us in the same vein. In the Akashic Records we learn that this is the law. Having adjusted our grid, we become magnets for love and support. Anything less cannot enter our inner realms; instead, it falls away.

The Gatekeeper of Our Best Selves

Another dynamic that occurs and has the power to alter our Light Grid relates to the gatekeeper function of the Innermost

Self. While destructive patterns are being created and encoded in the grid, the gatekeeper plays its part. The wounded, vulnerable parts of ourselves act to protect our inner riches, safeguarding our greatest gifts. In moments of distress, real or imagined, the innermost part of our being takes action, gathering up whatever is most valuable to us at the time in order to preserve it. While we may believe that our best traits, insights, and energies are lost to us, they are not. They're merely in storage, awaiting release. Once we forge an intimate connection with our Innermost Self, we can access them again.

You do not have to have a highly dysfunctional childhood to become disconnected from your Innermost Self. You can be a child who is curious about life, connects with people, is highly creative, and possesses clear intuition along with other wonderful resources in your possession. However, when you experience any kind of difficulty, even with rich personal resources, your relationship with your resources alters. In moments of distress, these positive aspects of you get hidden away until it is safe for them to resurface. The problem is that in our interior world, time is not dominant, so we cannot tell when it is safe to bring these aspects of ourselves back out into the open. Impactful moments take precedence and capture our attention, whether they occurred forty years ago or just this morning. But when we examine them in the Records, we can regain direct contact with all of the beautiful facets of ourselves we have buried for protection and release them to come to our aid. Ultimately, we come to see that meeting with and befriending our Innermost Self allows us to consciously reconnect with and re-integrate our most precious aspects.

A dim or distant sense of self-awareness—a lack of clear perception of our Innermost Self—can take a variety of forms and create a range of symptoms. We will have difficulty hearing ourselves, knowing what we mean, knowing what we want, and even knowing our preferences. Without connection to the wisdom inherent in the Innermost Self, we may be indecisive, or we may move in the other direction, making choices without giving serious thought to the consequences. Either response can leave us with undue focus on the opinions of others and a clingy dependence on their approval. Maintaining satisfying relationships is troublesome when we are in this condition. We may develop the habit of looking for mother figures or father figures in others, and we will always find that such dynamics are not enriching, either for us or for the object of our attention.

There is a better way. Meet yourself in the Akashic Records. It is time to become reacquainted.

Introducing Akashic Reflections

I offer the following exercises, which I call Akashic Reflections, to support you in making progress with your healing. As this is the first time you are encountering them, I'd like to present a little primer on how to approach them. There are a few different ways to use them. I suggest you try all the possibilities described here and then use what's best for you.

Review the Pathway Prayer Process before opening your Records for the first time (see page 35), and remember that it's a good idea to be disciplined in your use of the Records, to be responsible for the amount of time you spend in them, and to journal about your discoveries. This will help you go deeper into the Records and make it easy to track your progress. While you want to be disciplined in your use of the Prayer, you will find it beneficial to be flexible in other ways. Experiment with the time of day that is most productive for you. Some people do great work in the morning; others do better in the evening. Try both and see what works for you. I think it is very supportive to have a regular, designated place to do inner work. As you spend your time in this location, it becomes charged with the Akashic energies, which in turn nurture your process. Pay attention to which times and places are most fruitful.

As you review the Akashic Reflections, you will notice that there are a series of questions or ideas to bring to your Records. Let yourself experiment with these. With some of the topics, you may find it best to take one question at a time to your Records: it may best serve you to go slowly rather than to plow through. If you are moved to tackle more than one at a time, try that and see how it works for you. The key is noticing how you are responding to the questions. If you find yourself energized and want to press on through the material, by all means go for it. This is your healing process and you will be able to discern a pace and rhythm that work for you.

As a general rule, don't settle for clichés in your Records. If an answer seems superficial, ask for more. For example, if you ask about your purpose in life and your response is that you are a healing presence or a blessing to your family and friends, this is nice to hear, but vague. Go ahead and probe for more. What kind of healing presence? What does it mean to be a blessing to others? What type of healing am I here to do—is there a way to develop this quality? Is there something for me to do about this, or is this just something to know? It is perfectly appropriate to press into your Records for fuller, more detailed information. Ask and you *will* receive.

Keep in mind that this is a progression toward healing; it is alive and changing. You will grow and develop as you do this work, and the way you relate to various subject areas will shift as well. Let yourself go with your own inner flow. Some sessions may be quick and easy, others a bit more tedious and painstaking. Don't judge your experience. Remember the absolutes of the Akasha: "Judge Not," "Fear Not," "Resist Not."

Some of the questions may set off explosions, as if you've pulled the pin on a hand grenade. Others may net nothing; they may seem flat or inert to you. Don't be surprised if you return to these at a later time and find them highly charged, or if those that previously held such power have now become dull. The most important principle of all is to give yourself a chance. This is not a race. There is no set time to cross the finish line having worked through all the questions.

Your results are based on your efforts. Minimal efforts yield minimal results. Dedicated, continued attention brings about rich returns. It's up to you. Give yourself the opportunity to discover what really works for you with regard to your own healing through the Records. If you open to the best possible ways to work in your unique Records, you cannot do this incorrectly. Don't be surprised if you don't progress in a perfectly straight line—this journey takes place on a winding road running through a varied landscape. The only way to stray off the path is to stop doing the work altogether. All of your great efforts and focused attention will keep you squarely on the road to successful healing.

◆

Akashic Reflections

Open Your Records

- Ask your Masters, Teachers, and Loved Ones to bring to mind a current difficulty you are experiencing that is rooted in the issue of lack of self-awareness. Remember to be as specific as you can in describing this current life difficulty. Your story is what actually happened, and it is never vague. Review the situation and why it is trouble- some for you. The Akashic Records hold the story of your soul through time, so very clearly relating the story of your experience is of great value here. Spend about fifteen minutes receiving whatever makes its presence known.

Close Your Records

- If you wish, write down anything about your experi- ence you may want to revisit at a later time.

Open Your Records

- Ask your Masters, Teachers, and Loved Ones to help you see the ways in which you have been asleep to yourself or unaware of your Innermost Self.

- With their understanding and compassionate perspective, ask them to reveal to you how this lack of awareness has affected you in your everyday life. Make note of what they "seem" to be suggesting, whether you discern it through images or your feelings. Do not evaluate. Simply jot down what you are getting.

Close Your Records

CHAPTER FIVE

Self-Acceptance:
The Spiritual Practice of
Unconditional Self-Love

In the realm of spiritual healing there are two related dimensions: the inner and the outer. These two travel together as aspects of a whole unit. Permanent change requires that both be fully engaged. A shift in only one dimension may produce some relief or a temporary adjustment within us but it will be incomplete and impermanent. The goal here is full release from all obstructions to experiencing our own goodness. Achieving this goal necessitates a thorough approach, which is the nature of our work together.

Inner change without corresponding congruent action will not endure in the physical world. There must be an external, tangible expression of the inner shift in order for it to become anchored as the new standard of who we are. Similarly, external change that is not supported by a corresponding inner reality will fade. Even the simplest behavioral changes or new activities, if not resonant with internal perceptions and consciousness, cannot succeed for any length of time, even with the best intentions and a Herculean force of will. If we are to successfully navigate from feeling stuck and dissatisfied to achieving inner peace and fulfillment, both aspects of our lives must move in tandem.

Tapping the Infinite Inner Reservoir of Self-Acceptance

There is within each of us a reservoir that has both the capacity and the responsibility to provide us with complete and unreserved emotional acceptance. Tolerating and "putting up with" do not even register in this dimension: I am speaking instead about infinite acceptance and true appreciation of who and how we are—and are not.

Judgment and condemnation do not exist in this part of yourself; here, you can do no wrong—ever. You can behave or think in a way that is completely ridiculous; you can have a short temper or a foul attitude or decide to bathe in self-pity; you can behave in a wholly inappropriate manner. Nonetheless, this part of yourself will rise up and say, "Of course you feel that way!" or "Of course you did that!" or "Of course you did not do that!" Notice that this inner reserve says, "You feel that way" not "I feel that way." It's like the voice of a kind and loving parent comforting a child. There may be times when it emerges differently, as a voice more fully your own: "Of course I feel like this!" Whichever way it is expressed, this radical kind of Self-Acceptance is a powerful antidote to any and every form of self-condemnation.

At the moment you articulate this "Of course!" sentiment to yourself, your difficulty begins to dissolve, and any resistance you may have toward yourself and your self-expression becomes disempowered. It's like yanking out the plug on the energy feeding the negativity. This understanding, applied consciously, disables the internal scaffolding of self-rejection. As words of complete acceptance well up—whether spoken as by a caring guardian or by your very self validating your experience—internal rigidity softens, stress drains away, and space opens up within that allows you to see and know yourself more clearly than before.

We know how self-judgments and admonitions can take charge. When we demonstrate our humanity and our imperfections, or we fail to meet our own expectations, we can respond to ourselves in many less-than-helpful ways: becoming frustrated, angry, or dismissive. Our internal conversation becomes harsh, disrespectful, patronizing, or ridiculing: "Stop it!" "You fool." "Get over it." "How could you?" "Why didn't you?" The litany is lengthy, and it can run incessantly.

What happens energetically when we berate ourselves is that our distress gets locked inside of us. Rejection and resistance act like crazy glue—emphasis on the "crazy"—between the emotions and energy body. Negative responses fix the object of their scorn in place, where it becomes petrified, and we become hostage to the very thing we disdain. If we sit with this harsh self-talk long enough, we absorb it into our system and eventually become what we condemn. This is extremely painful to endure.

If rejection and resistance are crazy glue between the emotional body and the energy field, acceptance and appreciation are Teflon. When we actively engage in Self-Acceptance and Self-Appreciation, our responses to our thoughts and actions flow through us, keeping us in our present reality. Any responses we don't prefer can simply arise and then pass—we can have our experience and be done with it. This requires a certain fearlessness, however, as well as a non-judgmental stance. Fortunately for us, these qualities are available in abundance within our Records: they are among the governing principles of the Akasha. If we find that we are unable to muster a little Self-Acceptance on our own, we can find more than enough of it within our Records and use that until we can cultivate it within ourselves.

How do you apply unconditional Self-Acceptance? It is surprisingly simple—in fact, I have already described it. No matter what is happening with you, no matter what your response to any person, situation, or event, no matter how petty or immature you are in any given moment, respond to yourself in the language of the great reservoir of Self-Acceptance within you: "Of course!" "Of course you feel that way." "Of course I did that." "Of course I didn't do this other thing." "Of course that's what you are thinking." While it is an utterly simple thing to do, it is also a spiritual practice—the practice of extending unconditional love to yourself. Engaging in this pattern of thought moves unconditional self-love from the arena of "nice idea" into one of active use. Because we are here on the Earth plane—the plane of incarnation, or making ideas physical—this is the perfect way to manifest our true feelings of unconditional self-love. It is an act of creating the world in which we want to live. In the long run, we can develop the ability to extend this practical acceptance to others as well. But for now, our first step in healing through the Akashic Records is to focus on ourselves.

Perhaps a brief discussion of spiritual practice is in order at this juncture—maybe the response just described seems too easy to qualify as one. A spiritual practice is any action, behavior, or thought that, when deliberately repeated, supports our conscious relationship with the Divine and establishes a space within us for a greater flow of the vital life force. Really, anything we do with conscious intention that enables us to become more aware of our connection to the Divine Reality can be considered a spiritual practice. Walking in nature, praying, meditating, and serving others are some of the more commonly recognized spiritual practices. Exercise, yoga, dietary regimes—whatever encourages us to recognize our continuous relationship with Divine Life—can be spiritual practices.

Actively extending acceptance, compassion, and understanding toward yourself is a deliberate and conscious way to become more aware of the ever-present Divine within you. It is a way to move into alignment with who you really are, to reconnect with that most tender, vulnerable part of yourself. As you practice this way of relating to yourself, you will come to trust yourself more; you will relax and be more present to yourself. And why not? You're treating yourself better! You're becoming trustworthy. By giving yourself the kindness and respect you deserve, more of your inner truths will be revealed. By being wonderful to yourself through the use of words that are free from negativity, condemnation, and harsh judgment, you will reset the grid in your energy field. The improvements in your Light Grid will hold you as you continue forward with this new way of interacting with yourself. You will find that you are giving yourself what you have been seeking for years. And—paradoxically—as you do this, others will finally be able to give you what you desire. People around you will naturally respond to you in this way because your new essential pattern demonstrates how to be with you. Anyone or anything unable to cooperate with this higher standard will disappear from your view.

The conscious practice of unconditional self-love through the very simple response "Of course" will create an environment of acceptance and nonjudgment, thus enabling a more positive, honorable relationship with yourself. As your self-trust strengthens, as you prove again and again that you are a "safe" person, you will naturally embrace yourself and feel loved, cherished, valued, and appreciated by the most important one, your very own self. If you are safe with yourself, all other relationships in your life will begin to develop that same quality of safety. In this atmosphere of safety and trust, you will find all the facets of yourself moving into alignment with your Innermost Self. This is the foundation for the next step in your healing progression: making peace with what is.

The Key to Accepting What Is

To move beyond our current level, wherever we are at the moment, we must make peace with what is. Yet reconciling ourselves with realities we condemn or deem dangerous is not possible. Our perceptions of our difficulties—even the greatest of them—must be tweaked so that the thought of them does not stir us into states of agitation or distress. Ideally, we must come to recognize that all conditions and circumstances support our growing awareness of our own essential goodness. As we are able to identify the benefits of all situations and come to know their value for us personally, we can uplevel in peacefulness.

If we practice unconditional self-love on a regular basis, resistance and rejection lose potency. Knowing that we are truly *with* ourselves gives us the stability to grow further—into more love, more understanding, more happiness and satisfaction. We are always growing into expanded states of love in myriad forms. This is the great challenge and core purpose of our soul's journey through time: to discover our soul's perfection. We are always seeking our own good, engaged in a process of expanding our ability to love and be loved and releasing any obstructions to the fundamental essence of who we are. Ours is an odyssey of accepting and acclimating to more love, more Light, more peace, more power, and more joy.

Everything in our experience is designed to support us in this evolution, whether we perceive it as positive or negative. The question then becomes, "When my experience seems negative, how is this supporting me?" An elegant way to get to that understanding is simple. We ask, "How is this good for me?" And if we are in *extreme* distress, we ask, "How could this *possibly* be good for me?"

These questions are turbocharged. Let me explain how this powerful practice works: our minds love questions, and our thought processes will always move in the direction of the answers. It doesn't matter if the questions are positive or negative, helpful or hurtful. Our minds want to answer questions and solve problems—these are its favorite things to do.

Now, recognizing that everything in your life is present to support your soul's journey involves both spiritual practices I have described. When you are in distress, first connect with yourself and extend unconditional love. "Of course" is your first response. This always results in a greater sense of calm. Once you have settled down a little, ask yourself the question, "How is this good for me?" Variations on this question are "How is this benefitting me?" "How is this helping me to know my own goodness and that of others?" and "How could this possibly assist me?" Asking such questions will direct your attention to very real possibilities for growth and will reveal the healing opportunities hidden within distressing events.

Let me illustrate this with an example. If my child is sick, I may experience fear and exhaustion. But if I can view the experience from the level of the soul, I can acknowledge how terrible the situation is by saying "Of course" to the full range of my emotions. And then I may be able to move beyond some of my old patterns, such as reluctance or inability to ask others for help. My child's illness may be the catalyst that allows me to acknowledge the appropriateness of seeking assistance from others, to mature spiritually as a result of this realization, and to put the new wisdom I have gained into action. Perhaps at this point in my spiritual evolution, I would not have been able to reach out to others on my own behalf, but my distress over my child's illness enables me to take that vital step. And so my question "How could this possibly benefit me?" is answered.

I realize that this may seem awkward at first, but if you are persistent in formulating these ideas as you encounter difficulties—even the baffling kind that seem senseless—you will find great insight and powerful awareness. This is tremendously liberating, and raising such questions is energizing for a couple of reasons. First, it puts you into a receptive state, which is essential if you are to grow beyond your current level. To move out of a stuck place, you have to be open to new ideas; your old ideas got you stuck in the first place. Second, while not knowing the answers yet can be uncomfortable, questioning offers possibility. When you don't understand what is happening or how to handle yourself in a situation, admitting so propels you into a place where new solutions, perspectives, and probabilities can be revealed. The inquiry itself—posing a new question—will carry you away from your old patterns, particularly those involving victimization, and bring you to increased personal responsibility and empowerment.

One of the greatest challenges for those who are awakening is being able to find the Light in any and all situations. This sounds like a lovely spiritual notion. But in fact, it is actually quite demanding. Once achieved, it is remarkably freeing. We can agree that it takes little to find the Light and love in times of peace and harmony. But it can seem like one of the labors of Hercules to find Light and love when your heart is broken, when you have lost your job, when you have suffered injustice or physical injury. Rest assured, these dire situations offer the ultimate opportunity for your soul's growth—to seek and find the Light under any conditions, to stand strong in the midst of any storm and to know true peace. Such are the privileges and responsibilities of those of us who are awakening in our time.

Asking, "How is this good for me?" "How can this benefit me?" "How can this help me know my own goodness and the goodness of others?" allows you to see all that is conspiring to help you become aware of your true nature. Understand that this is different from asking yourself *what* lessons you can learn through this difficulty. There is only one lesson to learn—the inherent goodness of your own soul. Ultimately, this is what all the lesser learnings point toward. We already know that the best answer to *what* is to eventually discover our own perfection, our Divine nature. When the Akashic Records offer answers to *how,* it helps us move toward this ultimate realization.

It is also important that when we ask "How is this good for me?" we take personal responsibility for our experience. We must recognize that everything is in our experience as a result of our consciousness. This is not an indictment; it is not a negative, it just is. When we consider that whatever is unfolding is for our support, for our benefit, we find it easier to take responsibility. And this shifts us to the center point of power within ourselves, where we can receive the blessings of everything life has to offer and graciously decline anything that is not a resonant connection. The absence of resistance, rejection, and judgment enables us to move into the flow of what is happening, rather than being bent or broken by our human experience. Instead, we locate our inner Light and hang on for the ride.

Another series of Akashic Reflections follows. These present opportunities for you to experiment with the application of the ideas we have just discussed. All address the same theme of unconditional self-love, from varying angles. You may find one of them very helpful at this point in your life, and the others not so much. This is to be expected. Try them all over a period of time. Pay attention to what rings true for you, and go with that practice. You are being led into a deeper relationship with yourself, and this is an opportunity to follow your inner guidance. Through it, you will attain the results that are best for you.

❖

Akashic Reflections

Open Your Records

* You have within you an infinite reservoir of unconditional self-love and appreciation for who you are. Ask your Masters, Teachers, and Loved Ones to help you make contact with that realm. The Akashic Records are a Bridge of Light that can safely transport you to the very core of your being. While in this dimension, take some time to identify the qualities of self-appreciation and self-love that are essential both to the fabric of your soul and to the atmosphere of the Akasha. Make note of these qualities. Let yourself be

immersed in them. They are within you; they are a part of you.

Close Your Records

Open Your Records

- Take a moment to allow yourself to experience total self-love. If your love for yourself does not feel complete, notice whether you feel more of it than usual. Make note of how this is for you. Notice some of the specifics of your experience. In particular, look to see what types or styles of nurturing, caregiving, and acceptance are easiest for you to receive from yourself. For example, you may be moved to treat yourself gently and decide to draw a hot bath. Or you may feel like cheering yourself on, saying, "You can do it!" Pay attention to this response.

Close Your Records

Open Your Records

- Use the Akashic Records as a laser beam illuminating your richest spiritual reserves, and ask your Masters, Teachers, and Loved Ones to help you locate that realm within where you have complete understanding and compassion for yourself. This is the zone where you can say "Of course" in response to anything and everything you do. Let them assist you in achieving this.

Close Your Records

Open Your Records

- Bring to mind a current situation about which you feel annoyed, irritated, impatient, or otherwise upset with yourself. Present this to the "Of course" zone. Let yourself experience extending infinite kindness to yourself.

Close Your Records

Open Your Records

- Now bring to mind a particularly difficult situation that you find baffling or senseless. With the guidance of your Masters, Teachers, and Loved Ones, ask how it is good for you. Ask them to help you see what is happening as beneficial for you or as supporting you in knowing the essential goodness of your being. You may want to run a few different situations past them to see how this turbocharged healing question can work to shift your perception.

Close Your Records

Open Your Records

- Ask your Masters, Teachers, and Loved Ones to reveal a situation in your life today that could be radically healed by extending active and unabashed love to yourself. Even if you are simply pretending to give yourself love at this point, let them take you to the place within where you have only love, honor, and respect for yourself. Be immersed in that possibility.

Ask your Masters, Teachers, and Loved Ones to show you, tell you, or help you to recognize how your problem could be resolved by extending love to yourself.

Close Your Records

Homework

Here is some homework that will let you road-test these practices. Keep in mind that unconditional Self-Acceptance is not just a lovely notion; it is a powerful spiritual practice. Under all circumstances, no matter what you do or don't do, no matter how you feel, your mantra is always: "Of course!" "Of course, my dear." "Of course you feel that way." "Of course you did that." "Of course you think that." "Of course you didn't." "Of course, of course, of course." The idea is to affirm yourself, to make yourself right. Even if you believe your response is "wrong"—crying in front of others, or raising your voice in anger, for example—your own loving acceptance of yourself will dissolve this error and you will naturally self-correct.

I invite you to try this spiritual practice daily for one week. Whenever a self-critical thought arises, meet it with the antidote: "Of course." Ensure that you can do no wrong in your own eyes. No matter what you say or do, and no matter how you would usually respond, instead say, "Oh honey, I love you. Of course you said that. Of course you feel that. Of course you think that. I don't care what you do. I don't care if you sleep all day, I don't care if you rob a bank, and I don't care if you eat five chocolate cakes. I know you are good. I love you."

We are aiming for the realm of "It's okay." We are seeking the place of "I don't care what you do—I love you. I don't care if everybody in the neighborhood is laughing at you. I don't care if you push me away. The truth is, you cannot make me stop loving you. My loving you has nothing to do with what you do, what you say, what you think. I just love you, whether you like it or not. Whether you think you deserve it or not, whether you think you are worthy or not: that is not the point. The point is that I can't help it—I simply love you!"

◆

In the next chapter, we'll talk about the third step in using our Sacred Wounds as points of power in our relationship with ourselves. But first, for the sake of perspective, let's take a moment to review. In our healing progression, Awareness of Self is the first step, which is the realization that you are You. Then we move into conscious alignment with our Self through the practice of unconditional Self-Acceptance. Engaging in these spiritual practices produces a remarkable sense of reunion within. Feelings of isolation decline. Partnership with our Innermost Self is enriched and we advance toward fusion, the state of melding the infinite Self with all the fragmented aspects of our smaller, wounded self. Here, we begin to operate as a whole. The simple key to this healing milestone is Appropriate Action.

CHAPTER SIX

Appropriate Action

We are now at the third stage of establishing a foundation for healing our relationship with ourselves. In this phase, we fuse with our Innermost Self, and we accomplish this by taking Appropriate Action on our own behalf. In everyday life, this fusion manifests as an unshakable commitment to staying with ourselves; we no longer have the impulse to self-abandon to escape inner pain or to seek the approval of others under any circumstances. This naturally follows the progression from self-awareness to the practice of unconditional self-love, which activates inner alignment.

If you have been doing the work so far described for this personal healing process, you are already more capable of Self-Acceptance than you were before you began. You are more comfortable in your own skin. You have greater peace of mind and a sense of sanctuary within yourself. The unconditional self-love practice "Of course," when applied consistently and persistently, has produced a state of harmony, trust, and confidence. I have taught this practice to many, many people who find it a profound relief to at last discover a method that enables them to be on their own side in life. There is usually a honeymoon period with this practice, and it is to be fully enjoyed. You are entitled to appreciate who you are in this life, and this exercise is a key to that experience. After a while, however, you may find the practice incomplete or have a feeling that something is missing or there is more to be done—and in this you are absolutely correct.

The "Of course" practice is the inner aspect of a whole that also includes the outer aspect. Remember, to achieve complete and effective spiritual healing, the two aspects of ourselves, inner and outer, must be traveling companions. So now, through Appropriate Action, we consider the outer aspect of our healing.

Living and Healing in the World

Ours is a physical plane of existence, and for any change to be permanent on this plane it must manifest in the ordinary, in everyday life. We see in the Akashic Records that we are on an odyssey of the soul through human experience in space and time. Our purpose, you'll recall, is to come to know the perfection of our soul, of everyone else's souls, and of all of life—while here in the physical realm. It is quite simple to recognize the essential perfection of all when we are free of our bodies and liberated from the concerns of living in the world when we are engaging as spirits. There are simply no obstructions to our awareness of the truth while in this state.

Our challenge—and our opportunity—is to know this truth while fully encased in physical bodies and saddled with earthly responsibilities such as mortgages, mates, and children. This is our mission. To realize our healing at the fullest potential, we must manifest it as living beings on the planet. We accomplish this through action.

And so we must build a bridge from our inner experience of unconditional self-love to its expression in action, and then we must journey across it. There is a transition zone within us that supports us as we move from one realm of the fully dimensional sphere of healing to another. It may be helpful to think of this inner bridge as a protective zone through which you can travel from the depths of your Innermost Self out into the world. The protective nature of this terrain enables you to maintain a distinct sense of Self-Acceptance as you initiate the process of Appropriate Action.

As you begin to take action expressing your highest awareness of truth in the moment, your inner energetic pattern shifts from the alignment achieved through Self-Acceptance to fusion—the state of integration among all dimensions of yourself. Your growing awareness of this fusion, this melding and blending into yourself as a whole being, serves to fortify the process. In order to hold steady in our truth, we have to move into ourselves, synthesize with ourselves, and then express in the outer world the deeper inner relationship we enjoy.

One of the important understandings we encounter through the Akashic Records is that our human condition on

Earth is a reflection of our inner consciousness. This means that our lives—both the grand sweep of them and their seemingly insignificant details—are direct expressions of our consciousness. If we approve of ourselves and our circumstances, this is good news. If we have contempt or disdain for both, this is not such good news. Either way, we will come to terms, again and again, with this notion that the inner is made manifest in the outer. This is why Appropriate Action is critical to the journey of personal healing. It is the way we transmit our intimate perceptions of ourselves, others, and life itself into physical form. As we act upon what we know to be true inside us, our lives change shape to reflect that inner truth.

The Earth plane is one of manifestation, action, and realization. We are here to bear witness to our interior reality in physical form. This is our individual demonstration of the idea that all of life is imbued with Divine essence. One of our most significant tasks is to recognize that we, along with everyone else, are Divine in nature. As we act upon this recognition, we see the stuff of our lives rearranging to represent our understanding. Once we have made a solid connection with ourselves, one based in unconditional self-love and self-respect, we are then prepared to take action. This is an essential step, both personally and spiritually. Our spiritual life is not just a daydream; it is to be lived. It is the power of spirit that calls us off the couch out into life, even if we are not quite certain "how" to act or what exactly we will do. Once we become willing and make a commitment to act, the "how," the "what to do," is revealed.

Just as there is a realm within you that contains an infinite reservoir of unconditional self-love and acceptance, there is also a dimension dominated by the energies of self-protection, self-provision, and self-advocacy. This is the aspect that always says, "Oh yes, I'll help you. I may not know exactly how or what to do, but yes, I will find a way to help you." This is the part within that recognizes that it is not enough to sit around loving and comforting yourself. This facet of your Being knows the power and value of taking action on your own behalf. We all have this knowledge somewhere within us—it may have been buried or silenced, but it is there. Our great opportunity now is to use the Akashic Records to learn to locate this realm, access its energy, and harness this force for our own good. We want to be judicious and wise when using our inner forces: that is why we call this stage Appropriate Action. This is a process of discerning our impulses, deciphering our desires, and directing our energy into those actions that best express our inner truth and support our soul's purpose.

A Word about Inappropriate Action

It is helpful to identify the consequences of woundedness in this area of our Being: the wounds of "inappropriate action." Perhaps, for example, you have difficulty providing for yourself consistently: sometimes you are adept at making a living and handling the details of a human existence; at other times, you just cannot get it together enough to establish and maintain supportive resources such as health insurance, car maintenance, or even basic housekeeping. You may be uneven in your ability to advocate for yourself, to speak up on your own behalf, for any number of reasons: you may be unaware that speaking up is even an option, or you might be terrified of verbalizing your needs. This type of wounding may show up as an inability to pursue your life dreams, which may seem to you to be absolutely impossible to achieve. You may have exaggerated fears about venturing out into the world or a simple reluctance to be a regular person living life, having some successes and some failures and being witness to both. Wounds of inappropriate action manifest painfully when a person enjoys a rich inner life of grand visions, which never come to fruition because she is unable to walk out the front door. Many cease listening to themselves because the prospect of another letdown is too much to bear.

The Spiritual Practice of Appropriate Action

There is a practice, a protocol of thinking and behavior, that can help you out of such tangles. Much like the "Of course" practice, it is designed to be used consistently and deliberately. Actually, doing it will make a world of difference.

Here's how it works: Begin in what has now become familiar territory. When facing a challenge, take a moment to notice how you are responding. Then, no matter what that response may be, extend unconditional love and respect to yourself as you have learned by saying "Of course." This will help calm you.

Once you have settled down in this way, you can take the next step. Reach deep within, into the interior realm where the mastery of protecting, providing for, and advocating for yourself resides. From this place, take a few minutes to connect with the profound compassion rooted here. Listen to your inner cries for assistance and support, your critical needs, your secret desires, and the natural, loving response of the willing inner Self as it emerges with these words: "I *will* help you. I may not know how, but we will find a way. I am here." The willingness to take action is all that is required. You do not need clarity about *what* you will do, only that you *will* do whatever it takes to care for your very own self in the external world.

So it is a two-step activity. First, by practicing "Of course," you allow yourself a measure of serenity. Then, take a second to locate within yourself that courageous, compassionate, active response. Once you are there—however faint your perception of it may be in the beginning—listen for "I will help you. I am here. We will find a way." This is the key to Appropriate Action. When you know you are supported, you can find the courage to act.

Do not attach yourself to a particular outcome—that will obscure your next best step. Not demanding a specific result requires trust, and so we see that willingness and trust are both essential to successful practice. You do not need to possess a tremendous amount of either, just enough to move you to your next step. If either willingness or trust seems hard to muster, do not use this as an excuse to postpone this protocol. All you need is a smidgen more willingness and a bit more trust than you had the day before. Marshal them together so you can take the next step—now, today, in the present.

You will discover that this is much like trusting that your next breath will bring sufficient oxygen to your body. You don't need all the air in the world, just enough to nourish you in this moment. You need summon only enough trust and willingness to put one foot in front of the other and act.

The question then arises, "Where do you place your trust?" It might not be useful to place it in yourself at this point, especially if you have a history of disappointing yourself. Place your trust in a power greater than yourself. Interestingly, this does not have to be a "higher power"—gravity or electricity might work just fine, because these are energies upon which you can rely: they have already earned your trust. Or, consider placing your trust in the power that causes seeds to sprout with life, keeps the planets in their orbits, and keeps your vital organs on task. It is not necessary in this practice to get into a serious philosophical discourse about the Divine. Just take a look around and notice what you count on without concern. It is almost impossible to "surrender" into a complete unknown, and some people find it hard to let go because they are burdened by a childhood idea of a scary God. But it is very possible to let go into something you trust. The dependable cycles of the moon and the tides can be enough to help you to relax into the idea that there is a power for good at work in this life and you can trust it without a second thought.

To grow beyond where we are now, we must let go of where we have been. As the Records assist us in fusing inner acceptance with Appropriate Action, our inner wisdom offers great insight, counsel, and direction. This is the path of incremental growth and healing. It is safe, respectful, and real, and you can integrate it into your everyday life. As you listen to the desires of your own heart and take action to the best of your ability, you will find your path. It will be yours alone, a perfect fit, and it will make sense to you as it nurtures and sustains you. It will encourage and uplift you as you act upon what you know to be true. It will take you to your highest good. Believe me—I have seen it again and again—it is easier than you ever dreamed possible.

Remember: "Judge Not"

To accelerate our ability to take Appropriate Action on our own behalf, we must be free from negative judgments about ourselves and others. If we negatively judge the way in which others advocate for, protect, or provide for themselves, we will be prevented from developing those same qualities within ourselves. For example, if we have the notion that wealthy people are arrogant, dishonest, or slaves to their money, we may deny ourselves the opportunity to have all the money we need. We will never let ourselves do something we deem harmful, dangerous, or wrong. This is why it is critical that we learn to let go of judgments so we can grow in our preferred direction.

It can be challenging to suspend long-held preconceptions, observe how others do things, and seek out the "good" and the "right" in their actions, but it is essential. As we begin to accept the way others go about the business of living—even if we do not understand why they do what they do—we will become free to explore our own options and succeed at this business of Appropriate Action. Accepting the validity of the way others function gives us inner space, free from criticism, in which to grow. If we can perceive others' actions on their own behalf as good, positive, admirable, or respectable, then we can allow ourselves to act in a similar vein.

Now you have a sense of how Appropriate Action works: the protocol of "I am here; we will find a way" frees you to move on your own behalf in the world. And this allows you to move in closer concert with your Innermost Self, where you find the riches of intimacy, love, and respect. As you act, your energy level increases and you develop greater clarity and a better sense of direction. The more you accept about yourself—the inner and the outer you—the more satisfaction you derive from *being* you.

The Power of Movement

Deep within, at the level of our Innermost Self, we are always healthy, whole, and complete. Our work in this system of personal healing is about clearing away obstructions to this awareness so that we can recognize this core truth. The developed patterns of inadequate self-protection, provision, and advocacy exist in a layer hovering like a cloud over our core—they are not central to our Being. As we engage in the spiritual healing practices described here, the Akashic Light and the winds of truth blow away fogginess, distortions, and erroneous perceptions so we can see and know the essential truth of our goodness.

As we expand self-love, understanding, and compassion, we become these qualities in our world. And as we adjust to Appropriate Action on our own behalf—protecting, providing, and advocating for ourselves—we increasingly hold a place for such actions in our lives. What we do for ourselves, we become in our lives—and our presence becomes a force for good for everyone. As we take action to make real the deepest dreams and desires of our hearts, everything that is necessary to manifest them is made available to us: doors open, people arrive, assistance comes our way. Though we have begun without knowing exactly what action to take, specific steps are revealed and support comes, all according to our need. Along the way, fears and any other emotional conditions that have been thwarting our progress dissolve. They cannot fall away before we take action; it is movement itself that pierces our shield of calcified emotions. As we begin to act, a bit at a time, the shield collapses and who we have always been underneath, our Innermost Self, emerges.

On the road to a successful and satisfying career, we try a few different jobs or occupations. The process involves a series of actions. Making calls, meeting with prospective employers, putting together resumes, and working at various positions are all appropriate actions. One thing leads to another, propelling us through not knowing and confusion into right livelihood. Sitting home contemplating is only half the equation. Appropriate Action helps us realize our dreams.

To review, in this chapter we have examined the outer aspect of the healing equation: Appropriate Action as a spiritual practice that corresponds to the inner aspect of unconditional self-love. Most significant here is that we always have within us a dimension dominated by compassionate self-protection, advocacy, and support. You now have an exercise, a spiritual practice—"I will help you; I am here; we will find a way"—that takes you to this dimension, empowers Appropriate Action, and ultimately leads to awareness of the Divine Reality.

Remember your end goal: to explore your personal wounds as a point of power in your relationship with yourself. When you move toward these wounds and work with them, you uncover errors in your perception of self and your behavior. Inevitably, you also find the beauty, truth, and perfection of your Essence that has been there all along, patiently awaiting your Awareness of Self, Unconditional Self-Love, and Appropriate Action.

◆

Akashic Reflections

Open Your Records

- Ask your Masters, Teachers, and Loved Ones to help you locate the realm within where you are a master of Appropriate Action, specifically actions involving protecting yourself, advocating for yourself, and providing for yourself. Let yourself experience this part of your Innermost Self.

Close Your Records

Open Your Records

- Ask your Masters, Teachers, and Loved Ones to bring your attention to those you have known in this lifetime who are masters of these qualities: Appropriate Action expressed as self-protection, self-advocacy, and self-provision. Take a moment to appreciate these qualities in them. Ask to be shown what they know about themselves and life that enables them to operate in this way.

Close Your Records

Open Your Records

- Let's review our healing protocol. Take a moment to settle into your Records. Let yourself become aware of an area within that is very painful for you: it can be physical, emotional, or mental. Take this opportunity to hear and listen to your own cries for help. Hear yourself as you clamor for your own attention. Notice how this distress affects you. Notice whether you want to shush yourself or push yourself away. Notice how you react to your own distress. See what your knee-jerk reaction is to your own needs.

Close Your Records

Open Your Records

- This time as you hear your inner cry, try saying simply, "Oh, it's you. Yes, I hear you." Ask yourself what the trouble is. Find out what is going on. Listen to your own side of the story. Search for the problem. If need be, ask your Masters, Teachers, and Loved Ones for assistance, especially if you are becoming impatient or annoyed with yourself.

* Say to the part of you that is in distress, "Of course you feel that way. Of course you are upset. Of course it hurts. Of course you did what you did. Of course you didn't do what you didn't do. These things happen— it's okay." No matter what is going on with you, this is your opportunity to make yourself right. "Of course it is your experience. You can have whatever experience you are having."

* As you validate yourself, the enervated energy of distress will drain away, and you will become calmer. As you sit with yourself, you may be able to detect that there is a movement, a shift in which you move toward yourself. Welcome this: you are actually moving into alignment with who you really are, your Innermost Self. This is your natural state of alignment with yourself.

* Now, whenever you are ready, you can tell your Innermost Self that you will be happy to help, even if you do not know exactly what you will do. It's all right. Say to yourself, "Oh, I will help you. We will find a way. We will figure this out for you. I will help you. I will do what I can to help. I will do my very best for you." You may experience some relief at this point, or

even a surge of energy. What is happening is that you are in the process of fusing with your Innermost Self. Now trust that the next best step will be made known to you—and of course, it will.

Close Your Records

Open Your Records

- Bring to mind a difficult situation you are currently facing. Ask your Masters, Teachers, and Loved Ones to show you, or give you a sense of, how it would be different if you took Appropriate Action. Ask them to help you to know what Appropriate Action would be in this particular situation. Ask them to help you get in touch with your inner reserve of mastery in this area. When you are connected to it, take a look at your difficulty. See what Action you can take that will begin to move you out of distress and into fusion with your Innermost Self.

Close Your Records

CHAPTER SEVEN

Choice

We have arrived at the final step in the personal healing progression that forms the foundation of our movement out of suffering and into the joy of living: Choice. In this step, we come to realize our soul-level truth that we are our soul's first choice. We are who we are by design, not by accident. Every detail is our soul's choice: how and where we live; our strengths, talents, and abilities; our family of origin and the circumstances of our birth; our career path; our friends, lovers, children. These details are ideal for us at this time. The life we find ourselves leading, the personality we sport, the body we inhabit, every particular of our existence is organized to support us in coming to know our soul's perfection, to know our Divine essence no matter what our conditions or circumstances. In this phase of the progression, we honor our soul's choice.

It might be helpful to further explore the role honoring our soul's choice plays and the energetic impact it has within this healing paradigm. Accepting that we are our soul's first and best choice in this incarnation enables us to open up and expand the interior space we have for who we are and how we are living this life. Embracing the fact of our choice makes room for all the other stages of healing to fully ripen and mature.

When we arrive at acceptance of our most fundamental choice, the entire healing process reinitiates at a deeper internal level. This deepening fortifies the progress we have made on the other legs of our journey, which in turn encourages more Self-Awareness, Self-Appreciation, and Appropriate Action. We find ourselves consciously engaged in an ongoing process of increasing awareness of our Innermost Self.

Honoring Your Soul's Choice

By examining this issue of our soul's choice within our Records, we can discover some fascinating components. First, we see that our soul has chosen our human self for this incarnation as the ideal vehicle through which it will be revealed here on the Earth plane. Our current human self is the next logical—though not necessarily sequential—opportunity for us to become aware of our soul's perfection. For continued expansion of our awareness of our essential goodness during any given lifetime, particular human qualities are required, and are a part of the initial choice of the lifetime we embody.

In the Akashic Records, we learn that there are two levels of choosing. The first is the one I have described, the choice our soul makes before we arrive in this life. Then, once we incarnate, we proceed along our human journey making "choices." What we are actually doing is agreeing (or not) to cooperate with the original choice we made to be who we are, with all the natural consequences of that choice. The choices we face in our life journey are not infinite; they are well within the context of the original decision we made before landing here. We cannot make a choice that does not already exist within our probability: it is energetically impossible to move beyond the boundary of our options. We like to think that everything is possible and that we are completely free agents. The Records reveal otherwise.

We make "choices" to cooperate or not, to go along with or against, to accept or reject the possibilities and probabilities of who we are. During some incarnations we opt for a series of "choice points," and it may seem to us that we are making decisions or determinations that are outside of our realm of possibility. Actually, though, they are well within our personal orb. During other lifetimes, it may seem that we have absolutely no say in how our journey unfolds. When this occurs, it is simply because our soul has chosen for us that experience so we may discover that we do indeed love ourselves even during a life of "no choice."

The everyday choice we face as humans, and the heart of the Choice stage of the four-phase healing cycle, is the choice to cooperate with who we are, to become the best of who we can be in this life, and to live in harmony with our Innermost Self.

Let's consider some of the implications. If someone is an alcoholic, it may appear that she has chosen alcoholism. To the onlooker, it may appear that she is either ignorant or defiant. In fact, she has chosen to have the experience of addiction in this lifetime. It is a valid spiritual path through which she gains the opportunity to know that she is essentially good, no matter what form her behavior may take. At some point, perhaps in another lifetime, perhaps in this one, she will find it easy to decline a drink. It may appear that she has made a better "choice," but really she has no more choice in refusing the drink than she had when she was compelled to indulge.

An individual may choose to live a life of dramatic extremes. He may be born into abject poverty, for example. As he grows and develops, he may decide to get out of this particular hell and live a life of luxury. If this is part of the plan for him, it will certainly happen. If not, he will experience great disappointment and yet, still come to know that he is good even if he cannot make such a dramatic change.

There are lifetimes during which we experiment with the influence of positive thinking or harness the forces of our will to produce results. In other incarnations, we deal with ease and success; in others, we address repetitive failure. The combinations are endless. In each and every situation, we are offered the opportunity to recognize that we are fundamentally good, that we are whole and complete, and that everyone else is as well.

Choice is an essential and powerful step in this four-step healing progression, best recognized through practice in the Records. When you are there with your Masters, Teachers, and Loved Ones, you can access the zone of

Choice. This is the region where you can choose the qualities and actions that will support your increasing awareness of your own goodness. The moment of deliberate choosing within the Records is illuminating and inspiring, and must be experienced personally and directly.

Let's look again at our fundamental healing progression. The first step is Awareness of your Innermost Self. Following this is Acceptance. Appropriate Action balances the protocol, and Choice completes the practice. Accepting responsibility for the fact that you have chosen to experience this life—and the rewards as well as the difficulties that are part of it—out of love for yourself becomes the determining factor in the success of your healing.

The Protocol of Choice

Here at this stage—Choice—you entertain the question, "What is it about who I am in this life and the situation I now find myself in that encourages me to love myself more than ever, to love others more than ever, and to fall in love with life?" Earlier, we discussed the turbocharged healing question, "How is this good for me?" This new question takes you to an even higher altitude of Awareness. It leads you to consider the possibility that every sliver of your existence is part of a conspiracy, in the very best use of the term, to reveal the essential magnificence of your Soul. This is an act of consciousness that can liberate you from old ideas and archaic behaviors and will catapult you into a dimension of possibilities yet unexplored.

Homework

Your spiritual practice at this stage is quite simple. Jot down on a note card the following question and carry it with you for the next week, month, or even longer to jog your awareness: "How does being who I am in this life, with all the bits and pieces of my human experience, help me to know in my heart that I am good at my very core—whole and complete—as are all other beings?" Simply asking this question will cause a stirring within that will propel your consciousness toward new frontiers.

◆

Akashic Reflections

Open Your Records

- With the loving guidance of your Masters, Teachers, and Loved Ones, raise the question "How does being who I am in this life, with all the bits and pieces of my human experience, help me to know in my heart that I am good at my very core—whole and complete—as are all other beings?"

Close Your Records

Open Your Records

- Ask to see yourself as you are seen and known in the Light of the Akashic Records. Ask to see yourself as you are seen and known by your own Masters, Teachers, and Loved Ones.

Close Your Records

Open Your Records

- Ask to know as clearly as possible why you chose to be
  you at this point in time, *why you?* Out of all the potential people you could have been in the whole universe,
  you "happened" to choose to be you: why?

Close Your Records

Open Your Records

- Open yourself to fully embrace the fact that you are
  your soul's first choice. Notice your reactions.

Close Your Records

Open Your Records

- Ask your Masters, Teachers, and Loved Ones to
  help you identify the ways in which you are cooper-
  ating with the highest possibility of who you are in
  this life.

Close Your Records

Open Your Records

- Ask your Masters, Teachers, and Loved Ones to assist
  you in recognizing ways in which you are refusing to
  accept the soul-level choice you made to be you in this
  incarnation.

Close Your Records

Open Your Records

- Request that your Masters, Teachers, and Loved Ones guide you in seeing how honoring your soul's choice to be you in this lifetime is empowering and liberating. Ask them to help you to understand how the everyday decisions you make about how you live and express yourself support or detract from your original choice.

Close Your Records

◆

We are now at the end of the first section of our exploration into the power of Sacred Wounds: our Sacred Wounds as points of power in our relationship with ourselves. Through delving into our wounds, we dismantled our errors in self-perception, dismissed false mythologies about our character and essence, and discovered the magnificence that lies just beneath the surface of our distress. Here we encountered the awesome potential of unifying with Divine Reality. We traveled the path of knowing ourselves (Awareness of Self), experienced unconditional self-love (Self-Acceptance), and expressed both through Appropriate Action. We learned that the life we are living is our soul's first choice for our spiritual growth. Yes, we will benefit from continued practice, but in fact we have already arrived exactly where we need to be. Spiritual healing has begun. Greater awareness of our Innermost Self provides a new dimension of self-intimacy for our enjoyment and delight. We are now prepared to progress on our odyssey to the next level of healing: our Sacred Wounds as a pathway to peace in our relationships with others.

Our Sacred Wounds as a Pathway to Peace in Our Relations with Others

PART THREE

✦

Introduction

We are embarking on the next step of our journey through the Akashic Records: healing our relations with others. The first section addressed Sacred Wounds within ourselves. You gained an understanding of what Sacred Wounds are, how to work with them, and you practiced some simple yet profound spiritual exercises. If you think back to when you first began this program, you can see the changes you have already made. There have been adjustments within you and around you. Whether these have been subtle or dramatic, it is useful to take a moment and make note of your progress. Write down your observations about the shifts. Tell a friend about what has changed. When you acknowledge yourself and your development in this way, you fortify the energies that are gathering for your unfolding.

Because of your efforts up to this point, you may now feel more solid and grounded within yourself. This stability comes from being aware of your Innermost Self, treating yourself with the kindness and respect you deserve, and honoring your deepest truths through action. You may sense that you are becoming a Pillar of Light, a pillar of life unto yourself, and that is as it should be. Your preparation has readied you to venture into the world you share with others.

In this segment of our journey, we will focus on our Sacred Wounds as a path of peace in our relations with others. At first glance, using relationships as a path to peace may seem odd since relationships with others often entail conflict, presenting huge roadblocks to our experience of peace. This is precisely the point. Our objective here is to realize how the wounds we have sustained in our interactions with others actually provide sacred opportunities through which we can come to know peace within ourselves and with the people around us. Realizing that this is possible is only a beginning. We may find that the scar tissue we used as a protective barrier can serve the opposite purpose: it can help us to connect.

There are two main topics in this discussion. The first is transitioning from resentment to forgiveness. The second is becoming liberated from limiting patterns—shifting from enslavement to freedom and empowerment. In each chapter, I introduce ideas for you to consider, present some new angles from which you can view the events of your life, and offer Akashic Reflections as in the previous chapters. These elements combined will support your transformation.

Before we proceed, let's look at the underlying assumptions. We begin with an idea that is fundamental to our work in the Akashic Records: everything that has occurred in our life has happened for our own good, for the purpose of determining that we are fundamentally good, as is everyone else and life itself. This understanding includes the notion that every person in your life has come into your experience to assist you in your heroic mission to love yourself and others in all circumstances. There is within you an infinite reservoir of love; the challenge is to release it to the point where you are so filled with it that it flows out from you to everyone you encounter.

When people are nice and life is easy, this is not a problem, but it becomes immensely difficult to let love flow when we find ourselves with disagreeable folks or in unpleasant situations. From an Akashic, soul-level perspective, we can see that these people have come into our lives so that we can learn to love ourselves and others beyond reason—to love not because we or they have somehow earned our love, but because we simply cannot help loving them. Our opportunity is to extend unconditional love to others.

Other people are in our lives to assist us in our growth. It is important to understand that their development is none of our business. They are not with us so we can help, fix, or change them. They are present so we can allow them to help us—to help us learn to dignify all people in all situations, ultimately falling "in love" with every person we meet. That is the sacred opportunity inherent in every relationship.

Understand that we are entering the thick of our program now. You are already familiar with the terrain. We will be examining who you have been within yourself in terms of connections with others. Your level of personal comfort and confidence in relations with others is solely your responsibility, which at first can be baffling. The challenge is to get with yourself, stay with yourself, and be who you are no matter whom you're with. You will learn to be unaffected by the behavior, words, or antics of others. Your task is to hold steady in the Light, not waiting for another to change so you can be happy or authentic. This is not to say that you should shut down and become numb, shielding yourself from other people's energies. On the contrary, you will become increasingly open, solid, fearless, and responsive, knowing that you alone are ultimately responsible for your experiences and your interpretations of them. Your relations with others offer you frequent opportunities to increase your awareness so that you are one with the Divine, that you are incorruptible at the level of your soul, the essence of your Being—and as a result, you have nothing to fear.

All that's required for this next part of our work together is some dissatisfaction with a relationship—any relationship. Now, you may have been mining this dimension of a relationship for years and resolved much—you may have only slight discomfort at this point. Or, you may fall into the category of being held hostage by an old wound that has ruled you for far too long. There is a spectrum of possibility with this; wherever you find yourself is the perfect place from which to advance.

Why Does Healing Take So Long?

As we enter into this phase of the work, it is important to understand a fundamental principle: Healing is always present in its fullness, yet growth into healing is incremental. It almost seems unfair that we don't realize instantaneous healing, but the fact is we usually don't. Let's take a look at this situation and see if we can understand what is occurring and why.

Our physical being adapts to its environment in stages, or layers. This gradual process ultimately enables us to fully integrate the unseen into the seen. If our wounds were to be blasted with massive Light energy beyond our ability to absorb this amount of energy, then we would experience all kinds of problems. In this situation, our unresolved issues would be activated, flooded, and fueled by the Light, and we would surprise ourselves and everyone around us with a surge of bad behavior. Radical change can be traumatic even when we are impatient for it or it is greatly needed.

In everyday life, growth occurs in stages. Just recently, our son got his driver's license, cause for a big celebration. Interestingly, he has known how to drive for some years now. He was physically able to drive by the time he was twelve and with his height, looked to be of age. However, had we handed him the keys at that point, disaster would have ensued. He had the mechanical skill but no experience in city traffic, Chicago winters, or sharing the road with enraged drivers. Over the past five years, he had the chance to mature, take driver's education classes, drive with a parent in the car for fifty hours, and basically grow into driving independently. Though annoyed by the waiting time to be of legal age, he realized that he had to grow into being a competent driver. This is similar to our need to adjust slowly to increased awareness of the Light, also best accomplished incrementally. While we always have 100 percent potential, it is for our benefit to grow into it bit by bit.

The fact that we have to adapt patiently into our healing potential is both practical and compassionate. The slow pace of growth is, in actuality, a blessing. This is a kind, gentle approach to healing, one that allows us to embrace, and be infused by, the level of truth we find in the Akashic Records.

And so it is that in our increasingly expanded awareness of our perfect nature—in this dimension, the Earth plane, the realm of incarnation—the most merciful strategy is the gradual approach. And really, what good is the Light of Akasha if we cannot harness it for use in our everyday lives and in our normal comings and goings with others? It must be integrated to be useful, and this takes time.

Consider human perception. The reason healing can seem so slow and tedious is that the dense Earth plane itself is slow and tedious. Newer, higher frequencies must pass through time and space into our physical plane. We can see this in the birthing process of all living things. Whether the birth is a plant sprouting from a seed in the ground or a baby finally emerging into the world, time is required.

So, as you enter this exciting new stage of the work, I invite you to maintain two levels of awareness simultaneously. The first is awareness of the fundamental truth that you are, at your core, always perfect, whole, and complete. The second is that through your work in the protective environment of the Records, you are growing into awareness of this truth at a rate that is respectful, kind, and manageable. Count on it!

CHAPTER EIGHT

From Resentment to Forgiveness: The Trek

As we grow in spiritual awareness, we become accustomed to describing what is happening as a journey, an adventure, an odyssey, or a quest. All these words convey movement from one location to another in the spirit of optimism, heroism—even grandeur. And they are all completely appropriate for describing our movement from limitation to liberation.

Consider, if you will, the word "trek." Hold it for a moment, and notice its markedly different feel from adventure, journey, odyssey, or quest. In the work before us now, we depart from our mission of glorious transformation and find ourselves traveling an arduous part of the journey. If you find these steps of the healing process challenging, you will know you are on the right track. While you may find occasional smooth sailing, overall it will be harder for you than your work in the previous section. This is true for many people because here you will confront areas of greater discomfort or awkwardness. Do not use this against yourself in any way, shape, or form: this trekking phase of your journey is designed to be slower going. I like to think of this leg as the valley of the shadow of death that we all must cross in one lifetime or another. Fortunately, now is a perfect time for you to make the crossing.

Remember that the purpose of this trek is your healing: transforming your wounds from limitations into sacred opportunities through which you can encounter the Divine Reality. We know that everyone has wounds. Everyone has a story—it's fundamental to the human experience. And you probably have a dramatic story: people with lukewarm stories generally do not actively seek spiritual healing.

Healing Alongside Others

It is significant that you are not alone on the planet; there are lots of other human beings present. In fact, to avoid others, you must deliberately act to isolate yourself. Our sheer numbers suggest that we are here to know, to help, and to enjoy one another— none of us can do this alone, nor should we. Since we are all wounded, it may well be that we are here together to link up, join forces, and be traveling companions on this great, transformational journey.

One of the great ironies of the human condition is that we are here to discover our soul's perfection through imperfect teachers: one another. This makes for a rigorous transformation, as we must look beyond appearances to see the truth. We must move beyond ourselves and even welcome relationships with others. We must go past the customary boundaries of our linear sensibilities to meet the unexpressed magnificence in one another. And just as we have needed to trust in our earlier work, we need to do so here as well—trust in a reliable and gracious presence that will guide our way and fuel our passage. We will glimpse perfection in the muddle of mortal weakness. This is a remarkable experience, breathtaking really, and it happens to all of us. We do not know when; we only know that it will happen at the perfect time. Our part in this unfolding is to clear our internal channel for Light and hold steady as we enjoy the grace that has been with us throughout lifetimes.

When we are in conscious connection with our Innermost Self, we are positioned to connect to the Innermost Self of others. We may even be able to reach the part of them that is hiding under scar tissue, once we have found our Light beneath our own crusty layer of camouflage. When we have met the beautiful and tender self that seeks protection there, we can no longer be fooled by the appearances of others' wounds. We are freed from the fear that has prevented us from venturing forth to connect. As we transform our relationship with our own wounds and discover the energy and aliveness that resides beneath the surface, we shed the fear that we will be contaminated by others' imperfections. The internal work we do in the Akashic Records results in greater freedom to acknowledge the full reality of ourselves and others, and a richer dimension of connection between authentic selves is within our reach.

And so we see how our wounds can become a positive link to the rest of humanity. When our pride has been pierced by the pain of entrapment within our woundedness, it becomes possible to reach out, ask for help, receive assistance, and offer support—to truly bond with others. These bonds create a zone of peace for all of us on the journey. We all lighten our load by sharing our difficulties, just as we multiply our joy by sharing solutions.

Personal Responsibility

When we begin to examine our interactions with other people, issues of personal responsibility and bad behavior arise, which can be confusing. It can appear that others are fully responsible for their actions. Yes, they are responsible for themselves. But we are also responsible for our own experience of their actions, just as they are responsible for their experience of ours. In the context of our work here, I encourage you to consider personal responsibility a little differently. Here, it means acknowledging and accepting that everything in your life, whether you like it or not, is here for you, for your growth, for your good; that nothing can enter your life unless it is ultimately good for you, unless it has the potential to aid you in knowing your own essential worth, that of others, and of life itself. You are the center of your life, just as I am the center of mine.

It is helpful to revisit a transformational question we are by now quite familiar with: "How is this good for me?" Be discerning here. We're not asking if it's good for us because we've been bad and so we must deserve it, or if it's good because now we can play the victim, even up the score, and teach the other person a lesson. The turbocharged healing question is "How does this particular situation, this relationship, this circumstance enable me to know my own goodness and the goodness of others?"

While we are examining this question in the context of relationships with others, notice that it hasn't changed. The question is still "How is this good for *me?*" Whether a situation or circumstance is good for another person is not your concern. Your ability to help or benefit others is always the result of what is good for you, because when you are blessed, those around you are also blessed. Their experience of the blessing, however, is not within your control—you do not get to determine their experience. From an Akashic, soul-level perspective, every person, place, and thing—absolutely everything that comes to pass, without exception—is in your life to support you in developing your soul-level awareness. When you examine a miserable situation or a terrible problem, and you introduce this turbo-healing question, your entire energetic connection to the problem will experience a radical shift. Simply by asking the question, you alter the energy even before you know the answer.

Recognizing and admitting that in some way, somehow, a painful interaction with another is good for you—that it is giving something to you, teaching you, growing you—allows you to move through the energetic paralysis that comes from perceiving yourself as a victim. The victim stance assumes that the world is a dangerous place, other people are to be feared, and we ourselves are probably rotten to the core. And this false understanding of the nature of reality acts as a barrier to accessing the full power of life. The turbo-healing question collapses this false perception, and our liberation and transformation are under way.

Resentment

It is time to discuss a common obstacle to peace in our relations with others: resentment. We need to look at what it is, how it works, and the impact it has on us. Resentment is a condition of consciousness that involves unresolved and festering hurt, anger, or both. As a condition of consciousness, it involves our thoughts, our emotions, and our will; the combination of these three can make it a formidable foe. When they are in agreement, they form an energetic tripod that operates as gridlock—paralysis even. This sturdy tripod structure was initially formed as protection from further hurt or upset, and it is still effective in accomplishing this. But while we are protected, we are also blocked from the life force. We lose our energy and clarity, and we may get depressed.

For a number of reasons, resentment can be very seductive, even though charged with pain and fear. Frankly, much resentment is justified. Terrible things happen. We commit unspeakable acts of harm upon one another, sometimes knowingly, sometimes not. Hatred and rage can be strong components of resentment, and they are both associated with justification. It is important to recognize that being justified in your hostility and anger doesn't neutralize the consequences of these emotions. They still cause harm to the one who holds them; the injured party doesn't get a pass on the damage. Resentment is an equal-opportunity state: it hurts all involved.

From Shock Absorber to Barrier

Let's examine more closely how resentment functions. Initially, it serves to protect, and during an emergency it aids self-preservation in an elegant way. Hurt feelings serve as a kind of shock absorber—think of airbags in a car, expanding upon impact. They cushion us from the blow, but then, energetically, they lodge between us and our Innermost Self. They are absolutely effective at giving us some distance, dulling our pain. Unfortunately, however, they dim the life force as well. They interject an energetic moat between us and our soul-level Self, and we lose contact with all its marvelous expressions. Disconnected from ourselves in this way, we experience a marked disconnection from life itself: we feel like observers instead of living life. Our sense of the Divine presence dims.

As the energy of resentment settles in, it oozes into both our inner space and our outer personal space and begins to thicken. The cushion once filled with air now fills with a glue-like substance, becoming denser and more rigid as the mind and emotions move into agreement about the focus of resentment. Now it develops into a serious problem—everything we encounter must penetrate this rigidity in order to touch us. All our efforts to reach out into life, to communicate, make contact, and express ourselves, have to pierce this blockage. Given time, this becomes impossible: nothing can get in, and nothing can get out. And so it is that the energy of justified resentment—the thing that originally protected us—completely thwarts us. Most confusing and tragic of all is that by continuing to energetically feed this wall of resentment, we cannot have a conscious connection with the Divine. This, in turn, makes it almost impossible to register the signals the Divine sends our way—Divine guidance and inspiration. This is the ultimate drawback of resentment.

Causes of Resentment

It stands to reason that there must be very powerful motives behind allowing ourselves to fall into such a heinous state. This must be true because we love ourselves; we would not knowingly put ourselves into such a petrifying condition unless we were convinced it was for our own good.

One common cause of resentment is inappropriate expectations—of ourselves and others. When we have fixed ideas about how people are supposed to be, we set ourselves up for disappointment. The truth is that we sometimes have little control over our own behavior, and we have no control at all over other people. We have no say in how others do things, how they respond to us, or how they interpret what we say or do. Even if we sit down and offer a very detailed, specific outline of our exact wishes in the most loving and persuasive manner we can muster, the other person always has the option to choose how to act and they can always say no to our wishes.

Another aspect of expectation becomes clear within the Records: it is unfair to expect someone to do something they cannot. By the same token, it is realistic to expect people to do what they normally do. If, for example, a person has a history of panic attacks when driving on the highway, it does not make sense to ask that person to pick you up at the airport.

He may love you deeply, but it doesn't make sense to require him to do something he cannot safely execute. He will either let you down by saying no, he will comply and be in a foul state of mind when you meet, or worse yet, he will cause an accident. All are fertile ground for resentment. If you have a friend who routinely drinks too much alcohol, it is naïve to insist she not drink. It is reasonable to expect she will probably do what she usually does and overindulge. Of course, you always have the option of choosing not to be with people who don't behave as you want them to. But, it is unrealistic to expect them to act in ways that differ from their usual patterns or go beyond their abilities.

Another cause of resentment is loss. Loss itself runs contrary to our fundamental human wiring. The concept itself is so challenging, I am surprised we ever learned how to subtract! When we realize that we will lose something we have, or that we won't get something we want, it hurts. Whether we've lost a prized possession, a cherished relationship, or a dream we hoped to achieve, it can cause searing pain. Our knee-jerk reaction is to harshly judge the person or thing we perceive as responsible for absconding with what we covet. This judgment opens the door to trouble. We might judge ourselves for our inability to control everything or for being upset, judge others for letting us down, or even judge God for being unfair. The realm of loss is fraught with the potential for resentment, thus giving us the opportunity to apply the principle of "Judge Not."

Let's be clear about something here. It is absolutely appropriate to expect the best life has to offer. We all rightfully expect love, happiness, and satisfaction. What doesn't work is issuing a detailed prescription to ourselves, other people, and the universe about *how* goodness has to be delivered to us. We can go out into our day with the expectation of having a wonderful time, trusting that life will provide us opportunities to have the experiences we need, and that it will be good and we will be satisfied. But it is important that we base our expectations on *what is* and allow life to come to us as it will, placing our attention on our experience and our interpretation, not on the form it will take. Attempting to manipulate every detail and manage every nuance will not make us happy; chances are we will fail at such a practice anyway. Instead, the wisdom of the Records directs us to expect the best and be open to the ways in which that experience comes to us.

Self-Resentment

A critical component of our feelings of resentment toward others is resentment toward ourselves: all resentment has self-resentment at its root. We often judge ourselves harshly and against unrealistic standards—as a result, we stockpile negativity toward ourselves. After ample practice judging ourselves, being mad at or annoyed with ourselves, we build up a mountain range of resentment until our inner terrain itself *becomes* resentment. When this happens, all encounters with others must pass through the territory we have cultivated; and it is rare they will emerge unscathed.

We will do awful things as we struggle to learn how best to live—let's be honest about that. And this ongoing resentment, the sense of failing against an impossible standard, makes everything worse. The more resentment we harbor for ourselves, the more often we will find ourselves in situations that mirror it back to us.

If such mirroring is occurring frequently in your life, if you are surrounded by resentment, you can be sure there is resentment within you. You are being presented with a very specific opportunity for healing. This is a simple sign from the universe letting you know that it is a good idea to dive into your inner world and rescue yourself from the destructive merry-go-round you are riding. Now is the time!

The more self-accepting, understanding, and respectful of yourself you are, the less resentment you will feel and the less likely you will be to take things personally. You will come to know that every person, every experience, everything in your life is here to support you in discovering your own goodness, value, and worth.

Moving Toward Forgiveness

At this level of our healing work, our objective is to move away from resentment and toward forgiveness. When we become convinced of the futility of maintaining resentment, the combination of the Akashic atmosphere and some simple spiritual ideas and practices will make this possible. Once we notice that by moving through our lives barricaded by resentment, we are sacrificing our happiness, aliveness, and sense of connection with others and the Divine, we can become willing to let go of our resentment.

Awareness ignites the process; once we become conscious of the debilitating effects of resentment, it's relatively easy to decide we want freedom from its harmful effects. But we must also be willing to sacrifice its seductive aspects. Feeling justified is one attractive pull; it seemingly absolves us from responsibility. Resentment can also make us feel important and separate from others, whether for better or worse. These feelings are the ego's most popular tricks to keep us static in our illusions about the nature of life. When we are ready to let go of the perception that our suffering and isolation make us special, we will be able to enjoy the benefits of the Akashic atmosphere and proceed with our liberation.

"Judge Not" Is Our Touchstone

One of the three Absolutes governing the Akashic Records, "Judge Not," is primary in the transition from resentment to forgiveness. We do not assign meaning or value to what has occurred. Know that it is not for us to determine the worth or significance of an event. Acknowledge what has happened and make note of the impact or consequences, but also, we know that we are not responsible for arbitrating the ultimate truth of anything. Admit the terrible thing has happened. "Yes, he hit me with a frying pan. Yes, she ran me off the road." But then we refrain from judging. Living life, not judging it, we recognize that it is not our job to issue citations for bad behavior. It is deeply ingrained in our religious traditions that we have a responsibility to point out the awful things others do. Our educational system emphasizes critical thinking, offering rewards to those who tear others' ideas apart the best. Both systems reflect a fundamental misunderstanding. We are here to move toward the Light, to seek it in all situations and people. We are not here to find fault.

Negative judgment is a trap. It acts like a tight plastic casing that coats the Light Grid, a layer of clear, shiny material that locks everything in place. With our Grid sealed up, nothing new can get in and nothing old can get out. What remains must rot, and rot it does. We are left with old, stinky ideas, and unhealthy ways of behaving and interacting with life. And we will feel either superior or inferior to others, whichever our personality finds easiest to maintain its sense of separation and uniqueness.

We have a very specific opportunity within resentment. Our strategy for healing our relationship with ourselves fits quite well here in a wider realm of relations with others. Once you notice that something undesirable has happened, you can begin in the familiar way, by applying your "Of course" mantra. "Of course this happened. Of course I am upset. Of course I feel that way." This approach, which precludes any negative judgment, allows for the experience to dissolve instead of taking root. Then, take a moment to consider the possibility that the Light that is with you is also with the offending party, that the power that is with you is with him or her as well. Entertain the idea that the offender would not intentionally cause harm, because essentially he or she is just like you.

What is especially fascinating about this process is that as you cease the active practice of judging and evaluating yourself and others, you will open to a deeper level of compassion and action. Know that letting go of the need to judge does not foster complacency; actually, the opposite occurs. As you give up the position of judge, you free your energy to help you act in a positive way. You can move directly toward what you want, and this is immediately gratifying. Instead of moving away from problems, you find yourself moving toward solutions, and you have the energy you need to produce positive results. You are relieved of the entanglements that cause you to struggle as you try to stop what you do not want, whether it is taking place within yourself, others, or the world. Trying to stop what is happening is both exhausting and ineffective. This new approach I am suggesting nurtures you personally. It has its own energy, is more self-sustaining, and produces positive results more quickly than you might expect.

The Benefit of the Doubt Practice

This leads us to our next spiritual practice, extending the *benefit of the doubt*. I have been repeatedly guided toward this practice through my work in the Records. Though not always easy, it is a simple practice based on the truth that everyone on the planet is good: the essential, soul-level goodness of all people is not debatable. They may not be living up to their potential, they may not be aware of their own goodness, and frankly, they may not want to do either in this lifetime. But the fundamental goodness of every human is assured: everyone here is doing his or her best. This can be a challenging idea, but it is what the Records reveal. And the same is true for ourselves. We are always doing our best too, even if we fall short of our ideals, cause harm to others, or contribute to chaos and craziness. It cannot be otherwise. If we insist on holding back, saving our energy for another occasion, then holding back is our best at the time.

We are all learning how to live life, and that is what we are doing here on planet Earth—none of us has yet mastered it. This is why we want to extend to others the benefit of the doubt. Remember the Golden Rule: "Do unto others as you would have them do unto you."

The practice of extending the benefit of the doubt, applied whenever there is an opportunity to do so, will move you away from the yawning pit of resentment toward freedom and peace of mind. You do not have to be perfect in this practice, but it will make a difference to apply it consciously and deliberately. Any spiritual practice engaged with intent and awareness is energized to its highest potency. New behavior performed consciously anchors into your Being at every level. So, experiment with this practice. When you are compelled to slam yourself or another person for being a jerk, pause and extend the benefit of the doubt. Maybe you or the other did not mean to cause harm. Your own healing requires that you consider the possibility that there was no malice behind the event, that maybe, just maybe, what took place was an accident. What if you were in the other's shoes? How would you want to be seen? You would want to be seen as innocent, so why not see it that way now—why not extend the benefit of the doubt?

You do not know for certain what transpired. You can't be sure what was going on within the other person—her motives, her heart, her reasoning. What you can know is that she is, at the core of her being, good. Just like you. And her action, even if it seems terrible, is the best she can do at this time to experience her own goodness.

You are learning to ask yourself, "How could this possibly be good for me?" And that can be helpful to consider here. But when we're dealing with someone else, we add this practice: "What if he did not mean to cause me harm? This person deserves the benefit of the doubt."

The Elements of Forgiveness

Forgiveness is the pot of gold at the end of the trek. It is the star we follow, we reach for, and we dream of holding. It is the island of safety and security, the place of relief and release, the Promised Land in spiritual evolution somewhere past the valley of the shadow of death. How we get there can be a mystery. Some describe it as a cut-and-dried decision. Others arrive there via exotic rituals and spiritual exercises. A few will try just about anything to get to this state.

There are two main parts to forgiveness. The first is to stop feeling so hurt and angry. The second step is pardoning—letting go completely and starting anew.

Acceptance

Acceptance is an essential step to forgiveness. Begin by recognizing what has occurred and acknowledging it, naming it. The house burned down. Your spouse walked out. You gained fifty pounds. You don't welcome what has happened, but it did. Acknowledge, too, that you're all right: you're still here. You may be battered and bruised, but you're still alive. Taking this step of accepting and acknowledging what has befallen will empower you to move past it.

Refusing to accept what is in front of our very eyes is denial, and denying reality—which is life on life's terms—is spiritual suicide. You dig yourself into a ditch, and the life force of the universe cannot get to you to save you, to lift you out of your hell. So the shortcut to freedom is to accept what is, without judgment. And here's what this might sound like: "Yes, this horrendous thing has happened. I am miserable—and I am fine. I hate this, but I am okay."

Pardoning

When we pardon, we stop trying to extract some kind of compensation for the injury we have suffered. We forget about payback, about what we think the offender owes us. In the common-sense reality of everyday life, we need to adjust ourselves to the fact that the people who hurt us are not the same people who can heal us: the person who punches you in the nose is not going to be the same individual who sets it after it's broken. This is the simple truth, and we must accept it.

The Probability of Innocence

There is a wild card in forgiveness: the probability that the offender is innocent. This is not some kind of spiritual silliness, and it doesn't involve *pretending* the offender is innocent.

It is important to know that anyone who has done something terrible has done so in an attempt to take care of him- or herself. There is no mystery in this. Even Bernie Madoff, possibly the biggest scam artist in history, fits this category. While he was running his scams, it's unlikely he was thinking of ways to destroy other people. It's more likely he was striving to meet his own needs and he thought he had a great idea—the best idea ever. And then he fell for it, as did countless others who were also very involved in trying to find a way to take care of themselves. Did his scams really happen? Yes. Did he abscond with a gazillion dollars? Yes. Is he also innocent at some level? Absolutely!

We are all doing whatever we can to achieve peace, security, a sense of belonging, and meaning in our lives—and we are doing it as best we can. Sometimes, we think our best is better than it actually is, and this can be difficult to admit. It's more flattering to think that we're just being lazy than to think that our best is inadequate right now. But the nature of life is both expansive and expressive. We are always extending our reach, even if only a tiny bit. In the energetic realm, there is no such thing as going backward; there is only forward or outward from our own center. If we are surrounded by other people who are moving out from their center points in a dramatic and accelerated manner, it will appear we're backsliding. But our relationship with the whole of life is based on our moving outward from our internal center point, sometimes quickly and sometimes slowly, but always in the direction of expansion, alone or together.

The Benefit of the Doubt Practice and Spiritual Democracy

The benefit of the doubt practice described earlier in this section is a key element of forgiveness. It is important to remember when doing this practice that the life force that is with you is with everyone else as well—there is a great principle of democracy at work when it comes to spiritual connection. You can trust that everyone around you has within them the same access to the ultimate reality you do. The sun shines on all of us equally, and you do not have more or less Divine spark than does anyone else. What differs is the degree of awareness of this presence. It's like differing responses to a beautiful day: some people notice the beauty and it lifts their hearts; others are intent on focusing elsewhere, and the beauty eludes them.

This leads to a central truth the Records teach: never worry about others. There's no need to feel sorry for others or to be anxious about what will become of them. There is no need to send them Light or loving energy because it is already within them. If you are moved to do something like that, pray for yourself instead. Pray that you will see the other, especially an offender, as she is seen and known in the Light of Truth. The Light illuminates the good, the best, the most wonderful in each of us, even if we are behaving badly. When we see one another as we are seen and known in the Light of Truth, we release both ourselves and the other from those binding thought-forms. Once you begin to glimpse another in the Light, and to see that she is indeed good, it is considerably easier to give her the benefit of the doubt. So take the time to adjust your own stance, to see the other in the Light of Truth, and to ponder the probability of her innocence. This will dislodge you from resentment and propel you toward freedom.

Examining Our Judgments

Examining judgments is critical to forgiveness. If we have lost something, what are our judgments about loss? Why do we think or feel or believe that loss says something negative about who we are as people? Where did we get the idea that it is unacceptable to lose? If we have experienced a troublesome situation, why do we think it is so terrible? What do we think the event says about our value and worth? Exploring these opinions and beliefs loosens their grip upon us. In order to get beyond resentment, we must especially suspend our belief that we are victims and others are perpetrators. This will make it far more possible to let the offending party off the hook and to stop extracting compensation. We can let our painful feelings dissolve and reject the anguish that is resentment.

Apology Plays No Part

You might think that receiving an apology is essential to being able to forgive, but in fact, apologies have nothing to do with forgiveness or the resulting freedom. If you look back upon your life, you may see that you have at times wrangled an apology out of someone only to find that it wasn't the "right" apology, or it wasn't "good enough," or that you did not feel it was sincere. He may not have thought he'd done anything wrong, instead believing his life would get a little easier if he said he was sorry.

You got your apology all right, but you were still haunted by pain. And your relationship didn't change.

When a real apology comes our way, it happens after we have made amends or corrected an error within ourselves—evidence we have made a shift. We cannot clear matters between ourselves and another person unless we have cleared them within ourselves. All resolution in relationships occurs within us, not between us, following which reconciliation is natural and inevitable. Problems cease. An apology, then, is the icing on the cake—nice to receive, perhaps, but not necessary.

The Role of the Offender

Remember: The people who hurt us are undoubtedly here to help us transform our judgments and let go of hard feelings. They are here to teach us unconditional love by giving us the opportunity to love ourselves unconditionally in the midst of a lousy situation and to love them, too. It's easy to love people who are gentle with us, who accept us, treat us well, appreciate who we are, and communicate their appreciation to us. It is the ultimate spiritual opportunity to unconditionally love and respect people who are mean-spirited, harsh, cold, or scary. Rest assured, it's not necessary to maintain contact with these folks to take advantage of the opportunities they bring. The task is to make peace within yourself about them, about who they are to you, and how they are good for you in this life.

Until you make this shift in consciousness, such people will show up everywhere, coming and going through your life. The one way you will know you have let go of your judgments and resentments sufficiently will be that this activity will stop—hurtful people will no longer be part of your everyday life. You needn't concern yourself with how this happens: they will turn aside of their own volition, they will be present in your life but you will cease to be rattled by them, or you will be carried along past them by the flow of your own life. Until you drop your armor and release your resentments, you will block the flow—so why not let go?

It is important to note that you don't need to be in contact with the offending person to achieve forgiveness. The resentment you have is yours—and so the power to release it lies within you. Once the most intense energy dissolves, the offense loses its power, and what remains is peace.

Signs of Forgiveness

As you forgive, you will notice that the original problem—the cause of injury—fades in memory. It will not be erased from your experience; you will still know that it happened and that there were consequences. And from time to time, the fire of resentment may flicker again, but your experience of it will be much different. It will feel as though the experience exists, but in the distance. It won't pack the same punch, won't dominate your thoughts or feelings, and won't drive your actions. Your sleep will improve. You will have more clarity. You may find that your intuition returns, as if from a long holiday. If resentment has been particularly entrenched, with intense and extreme side effects, your emergence from it you may feel like awakening from a long sleep. This, in some ways, is the precise truth:

Because you have been so blocked from your Innermost Self, you have not been fully conscious until now.

A Word about Impossible Situations

Sometimes we find forgiveness impossible. If we or a loved one become the victim of a heinous crime, our feelings may be so torn, our minds so obsessed, our bodies so clenched against the pain, that forgiveness is just not possible, and we know it. It is beyond us to forgive. This doesn't mean we're mean-spirited. It's not a sign that we're unevolved. We are mere mortals with mortal limitations, and that's okay.

If you have suffered an impossible situation, this is an opportunity to call upon the God of your own understanding to handle the situation: to call upon the Great Mystery, the great I Am, or even the traditional idea of God as the ancient white-bearded man in the sky. Humans are finite, but the Divine Presence is infinite—let God be the judge and do the forgiving. As long as you recognize that this power is greater than you are, it can be within you or beyond you, or both. The circumstances you find yourself in are not a moral issue. This is not a statement about your worth. You simply need some help.

In an impossible situation, we see how our human weaknesses offer opportunities to know the Divine. It is evidence of spiritual maturity to know your own limits, flaws, and shortcomings and to refuse to use them against yourself by proudly holding yourself hostage to resentment. You do not have to resolve all your difficulties on your own, though we often think we "should." Surrender your pride and ask for help. As you place your problem into the sphere of your infinite spiritual resource, you will be relieved. You may want to take your resentment back at some point, and you may need to do that. You may start and stop in the process as you move toward the desired goal of forgiveness, sometimes taking it on and at other moments giving it over to a Higher Power. Know that the Spirit of the universe is merciful, understanding, and generous. When you are ready to let go absolutely to this Presence, it will be there for you.

◆

Following is a series of Akashic Reflections to support you on your inner trek from resentment to forgiveness. Remember, this book is not just *about* your healing, it is *for* your healing, which these Reflections are designed to facilitate. I invite you to explore them with an open mind, keeping your focus on yourself, as opposed to others you may know and love who could benefit from learning to forgive—it is impossible to transmit something you yourself do not yet have. As you do your own work, you become an increasingly clear channel for Light, and those around you will naturally be blessed. Trust that those you love are being led, just as you are being led to the truth. You deserve your own attention and care on this journey.

Before you begin to work in your Records on the subject of forgiveness, pause and investigate how you are doing with this healing process. Consider your actions—your behavior—which are undergoing change for the better. Healing may feel good, but it is more than a feeling. Here on the Earth plane, it needs to take form in the everyday physical world. Your work in the Akashic Records may bring about an abundance of warm, lovely feelings, but if your behavior remains cold and harsh, it is a sign that your healing is as yet incomplete. Take a look at your actions and ask, "What am I *doing* now that is different from before?" This is the best gauge for a reality check.

♦

Akashic Reflections

Open Your Records

Resentment toward yourself

- With the assistance of your Masters, Teachers, and Loved Ones, bring to your attention something you have done or something you have failed to do that is causing you to judge yourself harshly and reject yourself.

- Why did you do this—or fail to do this?

- Ask your Masters, Teachers, and Loved Ones to show you how your action or inaction was the best choice for you at the time.

- Where did you get the idea that it was wise to be hard on yourself?

- How have you been affected by this attitude?

- Ask your Masters, Teachers, and Loved Ones to show you how they see you with regard to this difficulty.

Close Your Records

Open Your Records

Resentment toward another

- Review with your Masters, Teachers, and Loved Ones an incident involving someone else that resulted in your feeling resentful.

- When and why did you take on this resentment?

- What convinced you that resentment was a good idea?

- What has convinced you that forgiveness is not a good idea for you?

- Ask your Masters, Teachers, and Loved Ones to help you know how this situation is helping you. What can you gain from it, and how is this situation better than any other for helping you gain it? How is this good for you as a soul?

Close Your Records

Open Your Records

The possibility of innocence

- Ask your Masters, Teachers, and Loved Ones to help you recognize the times others hurt you unknowingly.

- Ask your Masters, Teachers, and Loved Ones to help you recognize the times you hurt others unknowingly.

- Ask them to bring to your awareness times when you were certain that you were being helpful but caused undue harm to another.

- Ask them to bring to your awareness times when you gave advice to another and the results were disastrous.

Close Your Records

Open Your Records
The benefit of the doubt

- Ask your Masters, Teachers, and Loved Ones to bring an offender—someone who harmed you—to your attention.

- Ask them to bring to your awareness the person's motivation as self-protection or self-care.

- Ask them to help you see the offender in the Light of Truth.

- What will it take for you to give this individual the benefit of the doubt? To see that, yes, something happened and it was unpleasant or frightening, but the offender was doing his or her best and seeking his or her own good.

Close Your Records

◆

We have covered a lot of ground in our exploration of resentment: resentment of ourselves, resentment of others, the possibility that offenders are innocent, forgiveness and its elements, and the spiritual practice of giving the benefit of the doubt. These matters are all found in the realm of transforming our relationship with wounds stemming from interactions with others. Here we have the opportunity to move from turmoil to peace as we learn to forgive and discover the perfection of our souls through real-life interaction.

In chapter 9, we continue with the theme of using our Sacred Wounds as a path to peace, but this time with a different focus. We will examine the matter of our limiting patterns and look at radically changing our relationship with them so we may continue our healing journey, moving from a state of enslavement to a state of empowerment.

CHAPTER NINE

Freedom from Limiting Patterns: From Enslavement to Freedom and Empowerment

We are about halfway through our section on Sacred Wounds as a Pathway to Peace in Our Relationships with Others. As we free ourselves from our resentments and learn to forgive—and as a result gain peace—we find we have more inner space into which we can expand and flourish. The peace and freedom we earn through forgiveness is exhilarating and connects us with the joy of life.

Encounters with Limitation

After awhile though, we may notice that we are not as free as we had hoped to be, that we are bound in other ways that require our attention. This can be discouraging, because we may have hoped we had already crossed through the worst of our inner terrain. However, bumping into our limits is cause for celebration, because it alerts us to the fact that we have both grown and have room to grow. Any time we collide with internal walls and barriers we were unaware of, we can interpret this as a good sign. Such collisions are evidence that we are growing, expanding, and reaching into new territories of our Being. The fact that we still have some old, calcified structures within us is not really a problem. As we progress, we learn how to navigate these realms, pass through our personal difficulties, and press on toward new and uncharted possibilities. At this stage of our work in the Akashic Records, we stand at the threshold of profound personal liberation.

Many people doing Akashic Records work recognize this cycle. When we first step on the path, whether we're rushing at it headlong or have been brought to it kicking and screaming, we encounter a honeymoon phase. This period is characterized by countless synchronicities that capture our awareness, by amplified energy for everyday living, and by a sense of being immune from the grit of everyday life. Then, as we progress and our awareness deepens, we observe that we are not exactly in the place we would like to be. We have ideals, a sense of potential, and transformed attitudes that we thought would surely guarantee our catapult over the stresses and strains of normal human existence. But disappointment and disillusionment take hold as we find it nearly impossible to live up to our ideals and potential.

Initially, we may think there is something "out there" that is preventing us from expressing ourselves fully. It may be easy for us to identify those external causes of our failures: our parents, spouses, children, or bosses, the culture, our upbringing, financial status, level of education, physical appearance—anything, really, that seems to be in our way. For some time on the journey, we dedicate ourselves to clearing away the obstructions to our own well-deserved good—often with positive results. But even after experiencing some measure of success in resolving these external barriers, these thieves of our own good, we will eventually find ourselves back at square one: that space where we come face to face with the fact that *our outer reality is but an expression of our inner world.* This means that every external villain is a karmic mirror of our personal reality. Each and every person, situation, and experience is an expression of what is going on within us. Once we come to grips with this truth, we can totally abandon the game of rearranging our external world and get down to the business of permanent transformation.

As Within, So Without

As we work in the Records, we increasingly see that everything taking place in our everyday life is somehow connected to our inner world—including both the things we love and those things we do not like at all. When we first observe this, it may seem to be a fluke, but the longer we are in our Records, the more clear it becomes that this connection is constant and that every external element of our human life is an expression of our consciousness.

This idea is not new; we have already encountered it in our healing progression, and it is believed by many spiritual schools of thought. Within the Records, we can readily see the connection, and as we resolve our internal difficulties, we observe the changes in our circumstances, our reactions, and our experience of the world. This notion of "as within, so without" becomes very real to us. Upon clarification of our understanding of the situations we face, and as we apply the wisdom we receive, we begin to address our challenges from the inside out. They transform before our very eyes.

Many of us know the frustration and ultimate futility of focusing on the circumstances of our lives, striving to alter or adjust them so we can be more comfortable, only to find that we fail repeatedly. Working in the Akashic Records allows us to stop struggling in this way. Instead, we can recognize and claim responsibility for our own part in any situation and then direct our attention to our inner experience of it. We can then make improvements in our interior environment—and the best part is that the changes occur with considerably less effort than if we try to directly influence our exterior environment.

The Next Frontier: Freedom

And now, freedom from limiting patterns is on our horizon. What do we mean by "freedom," and why is it desirable for us? The kind of freedom we explore here is the freedom to express our Innermost Selves. This sounds simple enough. Self-expression is our right, and we want the ability to connect with the Innermost Self and allow our core essence to flow out into the world. We want it to flow unobstructed by personality traits, fears, psychological difficulties, confusion, illusions, delusions, or even physical distress. As we expand into increasing states of freedom, the human condition no longer hinders our personal expression of the Divine Life within; instead it serves or supports this expression. A radical shift in our relationship to our humanity is our reward. In freedom, we come to know our human self and human experience as support structures for the flow of the Divine within. We enter into a harmonious state between our humanity and our Divine essence. It is a magnificent possibility—and an attainable reality. In fact, this is precisely our objective.

Once we attain a state of freedom, we can venture out into the world with confidence, assured of many things. Knowing we are being led with everything necessary to sustain us on our path, and certain of our oneness with all of creation. It becomes obvious that all of life is for us. There is a quality of detachment in this freedom: We detach from the illusion of control, the need to maintain any illusion of it, and requiring very specific outcomes. Letting life unfold, knowing we are safe and no harm will come to us. Joining with other people, participating, and taking action or not, as our inner guidance dictates. Freedom makes it possible to engage fully in the life we are living, accept our interdependence, and thoroughly enjoy ourselves along the way.

The Records reveal that the state of freedom is not about the freedom to be selfish, to concern ourselves only with *our* desired outcomes and our gain. Actually, selfishness is itself a form of slavery. Here we are moving away from self-centeredness. We are shifting from relying solely on ourselves toward reliance on the Divine. Freedom is activated by true service, which is not performed out of a sense of obligation or with a heavy heart.

True service is allowing our core essence to flow out from us into our lives as a contribution. It is taking positive action on our own behalf, knowing that as we honor ourselves, we honor all.

Freedom has no attachment to particular results or outcomes. It knows that what is best will come to pass. Freedom requires trust, not in our limited selves but in the wholeness of life and the life force itself.

Discipline, responsibility, and commitment are all qualities that support us in moving toward freedom. Discipline quiets the mind and makes it possible for us to hear our inner voice more clearly so we can take action that is consistent with our inner promptings. As we honor our soul-level responsibilities through action, we experience a sense of liberation from nagging concerns about our contribution to our world, our purpose, and our work. We free ourselves from inner conversations and debates about our role, activities, and participation. When we recognize and validate our commitments, we achieve freedom from those activities and concerns that really are not ours.

Think of freedom as relief from limitations and restrictions. One of the great challenges we face in achieving freedom is living on a plane of existence, the Earth plane, which is noted for control. In many ways, we are comfortable with being in control and being controlled—it's familiar to us. Old ideas and social mores control us. Ancestral patterns, regional preferences, and political and economic forces control us. Religious and even spiritual forces exert control over us as well. Our very pulse is attuned to these structures at the deepest level of our physical selves. We are accustomed to operating within a mold made of cultural values, religious perspectives, and geographic and physical realities that define our path in the world.

In proposing the notion of freedom, we are introducing conditions in which there are no boundaries, no definitions, and no familiar pathway. We move out into the world in a way that is informed by our Innermost Self. This can naturally make us uneasy, because we face the prospect of not knowing how our energy will move or where it will take us. We may feel overexposed, and this level of authentic vulnerability can cause bewilderment. This is precisely why it is wise for us to explore our perception of the nature of the life force and the possibility of a reliable power greater than ourselves. It is immensely practical to explore these in the safe and supportive environment of the Akashic Records.

Let's consider another aspect of freedom as we venture along our healing path. When we look in our Records at our soul's journey through time and space, it becomes obvious that we are in the process of becoming more conscious of our own evolution and the evolution of humanity. This process corresponds directly to our expanding awareness of our own freedom. We find that it works in two ways.

Freedom as Energy

First, freedom is an energy that propels us along our path, an expansive and expressive force that is always on the move through us. From an Akashic Records perspective, we see that some lifetimes are more dynamic than others, but in all we engage with the energy of freedom. During some lifetimes, we may address the suppression of this energy and experience those particular consequences. We might lack the physical means of communication—we could be born deaf and mute—or we might be born into slavery. We may even explore the suppression of freedom through lifetimes spent enslaving other people. In other incarnations, we may experiment with freedom in its different expressions: political freedom, economic freedom, or religious freedom. We may be revolutionaries, actively pursuing new ideas and regimes. Other situations may find us expressing our freedom in order to maintain the status quo at any cost—using it to preserve an orthodox religious tradition, for example. Freedom does not always have to be used for liberal, social, or political positions.

Achieving freedom from want and hardship may take several lifetimes, and becoming free to realize artistic expression can consume another series of incarnations. As our souls travel through lifetime after lifetime, we all experience the lap of luxury and the bottom of the barrel. When we express ourselves artistically, we can be starving artists, accomplished musicians, or celebrated dancers, and this phase of our development will likely include a variation on each of these themes. The energy of freedom and our relationship to it is one of the major soul-level concerns each of us must face.

Freedom as a State

While it is a quality of energy, freedom is also a state, a condition characterized by an increasingly effortless connection between the essence of the Innermost Self and its expression in the world. In a state of limited freedom it can take a painfully long time to bring one's most authentic Self to the surface, and its initial expression can be awkward. But then, as we grow into our freedom and adjust ourselves to the safety and joy inherent in it, the distance between our Innermost Self and the world seems to collapse. It becomes natural for us to express our very core, and we do it gracefully. By the time we reach this place in our personal evolution, we have developed appropriate means of self-expression. Our vocabulary, our mannerisms, and our sensitivity to others become refined as we experiment with living in this state over time.

In the state of freedom, and with the energy of freedom propelling our evolutionary process, we can transform our relationship to our patterns. Our overall patterns—the combination of our soul-level patterns and our habitual patterns constructed during our lifetimes—serve both as supportive structures through which we express our Innermost Self and as filters through which we absorb and integrate the life force. As our patterns hold us in this plane of life, we become familiar with freedom in both its aspects: as energy and state. Once we have grown past a specific structural support within our overall pattern, it falls away, and we discover a more appropriate structure for still another newly realized level of freedom. This is an ongoing process until we arrive at a place in consciousness where we have no intrusions or obstructions to the expression of our Innermost Self.

Beliefs about Freedom

Through our work in the Records, we understand that we have to see the value and purpose of our chosen patterns in order to let them go. And there is another piece to this puzzle that is quite exciting. To let go of a pattern, we must first gain a clear sense of freedom and what freedom means to us. We want to have some notion of what's next for us in order to support our release of old, outdated perceptions. If we understand that we are letting go into greater states of freedom, releasing patterns that no longer serve us will be easier. We all like the idea of freedom, but in reality it means different things to different people, so we need to know what it is for us and what our relationship is to this potential.

The way we understand freedom will determine our relationship to it. If we have the idea that it's not such a good thing and may even be dangerous, we will avoid it, ending up trapped by our archaic beliefs and ideas. Since we want the best for ourselves, love ourselves, and are searching for optimal ways to care for ourselves, we can count on the fact that we will not let go and move toward expanded states of freedom if we have any suspicions about the nature of freedom itself.

Our Records are a clear and safe environment for examining these beliefs. Now, if I open my Records and ask, "What do I really *believe* about freedom?"—which would seem to be the obvious question—I will not arrive at the core of the belief. If instead I ask, "What is true about freedom?" or "What do I *know* about freedom?" I will be taken there directly.

Many of us are sophisticated about beliefs and place them in an internal hierarchy. We know that some beliefs are "better" or more evolved than others, and we will be quick to say that our preferred beliefs are truly ours. In the Records, it is easier to progress past our internal judge and evaluator and straight to the place of Truth. Here resides what we believe, in the form of what we think is truth. We hold our beliefs as truth, as law, and use them to guide our interpretations of our experiences.

So when we speak about freedom from limiting patterns, to what do we refer? What is the truth about freedom? When we are free, we gain a sense of room to breathe. We consciously determine our responses to life. We are proactive, make choices, and take action or decide not to act, depending on what is appropriate. This is the condition of being current with ourselves, holding beliefs that are appropriate to our stage in life and surrounding ourselves with ideas that are supportive rather than confining. Freedom from limiting patterns is about being awake and aware of what is true and accurate for us at this point in time. This kind of freedom requires taking a high level of responsibility, and then consciously moving in that direction.

The Need for Physical, Emotional, and Mental Accord

Our next step is to prepare our human vehicle for this multidimensional, multi-directional transformation. As human beings living on Earth, our whole self must be in agreement about entering into increasing states of freedom. Physical, emotional, and mental aspects of our being must all act in harmony. Each of these regions corresponds to a significant zone of our interior world: our physical self corresponds to will; our emotional self relates to the heart; and our mental self involves the mind. Each individually, and all three together, must be convinced of the value of freedom and also open to the inevitable change that will result from embracing this new quality of energy. If your mind is completely engaged by the exciting possibilities but your heart is just not in it, your venture into enhanced states of freedom will be terribly uncomfortable—and the potential rewards will be unattainable. If your emotions are flooded with inspiration and enthusiasm but your physical self is not ready—for any number of reasons ranging from illness to simply not feeling physically equipped for the challenge—you will not last long. Then, too, if your body is primed for new levels of aliveness but your emotions are in turmoil, no action can occur. Each part of who you are has to be reasonably comfortable with your next step into freedom if you are to graduate to your next best level. As you investigate each area to find out your current state of readiness, you must look at the limiting patterns residing within each.

The Physical Aspect

We have discussed the idea that humanity is the vehicle through which we come to know the Divine Reality. This interplay of body, mind, and emotions is the nitty-gritty of that understanding. We are here to road-test our spiritual ideas, to try them out in everyday life, including in the arena of freedom. At the level of the physical self, discipline supports us in gaining freedom from patterns that limit us.

Here is the opportunity to exert personal will so your body can indeed be a perfect expression of your Soul. From a soul perspective, you chose your body because it is the ideal physical instrument through which you can encounter the Divine Reality and express your individual soul. Every aspect of your body is exactly what is required for you to come to a richer awareness of goodness and to experience the Divine Presence as your reality.

When you work in your Akashic Records, it is helpful to take the time to examine your relationship with your physical self. Your body will provide much information about your awareness of your soul and your soul's purposes. This is an opportunity to take a look and see where you may be overindulging. An honest look at your relationship with your body reveals what you are doing or not doing to cultivate your physical self as a direct expression of your Innermost Self. You may find that you have habits that have left you with a body that is a less than ideal instrument for receiving Divine awareness. As you work to resolve this issue, you will expand your internal space for freedom. As your body becomes a more accurate representative of your soul, you will find it much easier to express the Innermost Self. Recall that we are talking about a progression here. Growth is always incremental, so take one step at a time. Cultivate your best relationship with your body, a bit more today than yesterday, and a bit more tomorrow than today. Yours is the perfect schedule.

From an Akashic Records perspective, all of our physical concerns—from weight issues to addictions to health crises—are intimately involved with our discovery of our indestructible relationship with our Soul and the Divine. As we acknowledge the services our bodies provide and what we perceive to be our physical limitations, our relationships with these issues will shift. If it is best for us to be free of a physical condition, it will dissolve. If it is best for us to maintain a condition as a way to stay centered in the Truth, that is what will happen. We want to cease judging our physical selves by our old standards and, instead, consider them within their soul-level context. This perspective can make a world of difference, allowing us to embrace a greater state of freedom no matter what our physical situation. Ideally, we will come to honor our bodies as Divine expressions, no matter what their condition. We will recognize that we do indeed have the perfect body to realize the Divine Reality in our life, and that everything about our physical self is evidence of life supporting us.

The Emotional Aspect

Emotions are a fascinating realm because they are so responsive, even reactive, to our environments—and so mutable. There are a few layers of emotion to be aware of. In the space of the Innermost Self, we have a profound resource characterized by love, generosity, compassion, and stability. Permanence and endurance are characteristic of this resource, as it is the "heart of our soul," the pure Soul Essence. This is our individual portion of the outermost or universal Soul level of our Being, and here we encounter the same traits and energies found at the universal level. The qualities of infinite love, kindness, and generosity swell to their potential in this outermost soul level. When in our Records, we can discern this as "as within, so without." We can detect the shared qualities of energy that comprise both the universal Soul and our individual soul.

This explains the centuries-long conversation about the location of the Divine Presence: whether it is within us or beyond us. In the Records, we learn that in fact both are correct, and our emotional body is held within the continuum of these two manifestations of the Divine life force. Our objective in this incarnation with regard to our emotional body is to align with both our innermost and outermost selves and to allow our emotional body to be metamorphosed into perfect harmony with both.

Each of us has a basic emotional profile; some of us are cheerful optimists while others are more pessimistic. It is valuable to be aware of your natural emotional makeup and, it bears repeating, to know that whatever your constitution, it was your soul's perfect choice. Within your fundamental emotional style, there is a part that responds to life, which can fluctuate rapidly depending on your circumstances. This part of your emotional self is strongly influenced by thoughts. When we speak of redirecting our emotions with our thoughts, this is the dimension to which we are referring. This is also the dimension which we are most familiar with, a realm that is notorious for being subject to flux and reactive to stimulation. Many of us have dedicated a great deal of time and energy to managing this sector of our emotional selves.

As we search for emotional peace and stability, two often-confusing situations arise. First, we connect with our Innermost Self and the Universal Self; we experience the amazing love, compassion, and richness of energy held in those dimensions. Yet, when we tap into our personal, ordinary emotional self, we find that it is mercurial, volatile, and not well aligned with either of the other regions. Attaining a discernible sense of the emotional greatness within ourselves and then experiencing its incongruence with our everyday emotional world can be distressing. Initially, this may appear to be an either/or situation, when in fact it is not—both are true in the moment. Our goal is to rest our awareness in the higher emotional state and suspend judgment of the messiness. "Judge Not." This will naturally cause these states of being to align and allow them to support the transformation of our everyday emotional reality.

When we experience our higher emotional state, great love and power surge into our internal world, stirring the pot. It's like a great light shining into a cluttered room—when the room was dark, we were unaware of its condition. Once the space is illuminated, we may find the condition of the room disturbing. Now, we might expect that our first experience of the infinite love and power of our Innermost Self or universal emotional state would shine right through our imperfections and out into the world. In fact, the Records tell us that this is the direction in which we are headed. But there is an energetic reality that must be honored. The Light will shine through us *as it finds us*—in our current state as human beings. If we are full of pain, hurt, and negativity, the Light has to travel through those conditions. By the time it crosses our internal terrain, it will have dimmed.

This becomes evident when we attempt to send great love and respect to others and find that they do not receive what we intended. Our limiting patterns have obstructed the path of the Light, and those on the receiving end of our emotional outpouring receive a stew of combined energies. We might feel misunderstood, and in fact we are—the recipient is unaware of our original impulse. When this happens, we have an opportunity to look deeper, find out what is blocking our clarity of expression, take the issue to our Records and work through it, and ideally move past it to live in greater freedom. Remember, each person who presents a challenge is responding to the essence of you they are able to discern. Listen closely; they are your guides on your journey toward greater freedom.

One of the most wonderful benefits of spiritual disciplines is that they quiet the emotional body. In the calm, our innermost love flows out from us and simultaneously allows us to receive and absorb more love from the universal reservoir. The Records reveal that an individual is able to acclimate to expanded states of love and grow in the ability to hold steady in the profound force field of universal love.

There are a few ways to manage your emotional self and allow for an immediate connection between your soul and your personal expression of it in the world. It is a good idea to do whatever you need to do to remain calm—not numb, mind you, but calm. You can develop a calm state as a direct result of trusting in a power greater than yourself. The deeper you move into this healing program, the more you will see that this is not negotiable. It is your choice to consciously engage in a relationship with this greater power. But the more you can relax into a force that supports you and the entire universe, the calmer you will be. Trust me on this: I have witnessed it in myself and in many, many others.

Pay attention to the flow of your emotions, especially when you are upset. Notice what gets you agitated, angry, or frightened, and then use the swelling of emotion to practice unconditional self-love. Demonstrate to the Innermost Self your profound love and commitment to yourself under any and all circumstances. And do try to calm down, too.

Detachment is another powerful tool to restore emotional serenity, and detachment with love works wonders. If someone has done something that stimulates an angry or scared response, look and see that she has the same Light within. Consider that she is entitled to her own path and experiences. Honor the choices others make; let them be. Being in the Records assists you with this. Greater peace and freedom will result. Attachment to others and our ideas about who and how they should be obstructs freedom. Don't let this exhausting habit interfere. Pay attention, and remember that your dominant, most frequent thoughts create the structure in which your emotions operate.

The Mental Aspect

We are living in an age noted for increasing awareness of the influence of our thoughts. We are also in an age of convergence, a unique time in human history when we have access to the wisdom teachings of the great traditions. Schools of spiritual development ranging from indigenous traditions to mystery schools to ancient wisdom teachings are available to all of us now, as are schools of the present day, including New Thought and New Physics. These can assist us as we navigate times of radical change and consider how to gain greater freedom in the mental dimension of our Being.

Ever-present thought patterns weave pathways of Light energy through which the life force flows. Becoming aware of what we think is of great value creates new pathways that are more appropriate for the true expression of our Soul in the world. When we place our attention on new thought patterns, our old established patterns weaken—we stop feeding them and eventually they cease to exist.

Consciously directed thought is beneficial, but not the source of power. Conscious awareness of our thinking supercharges our thoughts, which in turn accelerates the dissolution of old, largely unconscious thought patterns, providing for new possibilities. So as you continue on your journey of healing through the Akashic Records, pay attention to your thinking, notice what you think about most of the time, and make adjustments. Consciously replace unhelpful old thoughts with new ones that foster the genuine expression of the Innermost Self into the world. Align with those thoughts regularly and often. Together, your mental and emotional selves form a tight alliance, which can be your best friend or your worst enemy. Think, think, think, and with your thoughts, allow the dimension of your Innermost Self that holds freedom, safety, and respect to emerge. Relish the experience of immediate, authentic expression.

◆

In our evolutionary process we are becoming free from the limiting patterns that have enslaved us. These patterns have outlived their usefulness, and keep us bound to our personal shortcomings. We may isolate ourselves from our fellow humans, thinking either that we are better or worse than others. Isolation itself is a form of enslavement. The human journey is intended to be a group activity, with each person engaged in his or her own personal healing journey within the context of a larger group. As we become free of our self-imposed isolation, we can move into the community of humanity, the physical expression of the community of souls. We then become free to communicate, cooperate, and connect with our traveling companions. As we do this, we are able to express our Innermost Self for our own good and, naturally, the good of the whole. This is the evolutionary plan perfectly realized.

"Resist Not"

We have discussed the governing principle of "Judge Not" quite a bit, but since resistance is a challenge to achieving freedom from limiting patterns, we need to take another look at the principle of "Resist Not." We can only evolve and expand into increasing states of freedom if we allow our path to be what it is. We do not have to like it or be proud of it; we just have to allow it to exist without either criticizing or rejecting it. As we enter into a nonresistant state of mind, our difficulties are disempowered.

Acceptance is fundamental to dissolving resistance. Even if we can only allow things to be the way they are for an instant, it is a start. Any attempt to reject or push away what is in our present experience will ensure that it remains with us, diminishing our freedom. To expand the terrain of your freedom, to collapse the distance between your Innermost Self being expressed in the world, let your life be the way it is, let yourself be the way *you* are, if only for a day, an hour, or a moment. Try it, and observe the grace and elegance that stream forth.

Limiting Patterns

Permanent transformation requires that we stop looking outside of ourselves for the causes of our difficulties and solutions to our problems, and instead go within. Here, we find that whatever is interfering with our experience of our own goodness, whatever is preventing us from being our best manifested greatness, lives right in our own backyard. Within ourselves, we find deeply rooted limiting patterns of belief and behavior. External manifestations that limit us are expressions from within rather than causes from without. We must understand that restructuring our physical world helps only temporarily. Once we have achieved these insights, we become free to venture into our deepest inner spaces and uncover the true issues at hand, clean our own house, and live a liberated life. The challenge is resolving our limiting patterns.

Accepting the fact that, yes, these are our own patterns puts us in a position to get to work, and we can expect some positive results. We have tremendous authority over ourselves and our own inner machinery, and this is an opportunity to use it wisely. From this place of great influence, we can consult our Records and take a look at the life cycle of the patterns. Addressing resistance is an essential component of this work. We need to learn how it serves us and how we use it, as well as how to move beyond it. No one ever consciously and intentionally chooses a restrictive pattern with the idea of limiting herself in life.

The Nature of Patterns

Patterns are made up of repeated thoughts or behaviors that form an energetic structure through which energy flows. Once a pattern is in place, the life force within us has to honor the boundaries it has created. It recognizes us as the authority over ourselves; it will not push the pattern over, knock it down, or ignore it. Life has great respect for us and the choices we make about what factors enter our personal inner territory.

The pattern itself is like a web of light fortified by the combined efforts of our thoughts and feelings. When our thoughts are persistent and fueled by strong emotion, the web of light gets a blast of energy—similar to an electric shock—that further locks our patterns of understanding in place.

Then, when we add action to the equation, our ideas become anchored into the realm of ordinary life.

As we move through our lifetimes, we take on patterns because they are good for us and fit our idea of what "good" is at the time we construct them. They are useful for managing the way life flows through us; they provide a structure through which we come to know ourselves—or who we think we are—until we are ready to come face to face with our own soul. Our patterns form our identity; they are how we know ourselves and how others know us as well. They make living life on the planet convenient for us. In fact, if we didn't have patterns, this structure for our energy, we would gush like fire hydrants, expressing with tremendous force but without focus and direction. The patterns we develop as we move through our lives form a kind of hose through which our energy can flow in a way that is beneficial. The hose can be seen as a limiting structure, but it is also a supportive one.

Let's take a look at what normally happens when a pattern develops and how it goes from being today's solution to tomorrow's problem. In the course of my life, I have struggled with my weight, always looking for a way to get thin and stay thin. One solution I discovered was smoking cigarettes. It was wonderful. As my smoking increased, my appetite decreased and along with it, my weight. For me, this was the Holy Grail. As the years passed, though, two unexpected and undesirable patterns emerged. Much to my chagrin, I learned to overeat and smoke at the same time. Then I found myself with a nasty cough, shortness of breath, and all the unattractive symptoms of a heavy smoker. Smoking had become a problem, and I felt betrayed, angry, and upset. Emotionally disappointed and physically haggard, I could no longer regularly get a healthy lungful of air. What had started out being a great solution to my weight issue developed into a full-blown problem. I had to quit, which was brutal. Adding insult to injury, the ultimate heartbreak came after I quit smoking: I gained weight and had to deal with my original issue without the cigarettes!

This is the way the life cycle of every pattern progresses—there are no exceptions. It starts as a breakthrough, a new horizon, an open door and ends up as a restriction, a barrier, or even a wall. If we can skip the part where we get mad at ourselves, at the pattern, or at any other people involved, we can untangle our dilemma quite quickly. The key is to know that once we recognize that our solution has become a problem, it's time to rejoice. This is the time to cheer ourselves on to greater success, to pat ourselves on the back. Here is concrete evidence that we have grown, that what we once required is no longer necessary, and that we have expanded to the point of feeling the pinch of the pattern that used to support us.

Take a look at the patterns in your own life and you will see that they follow this very predictable path. It begins as something that sustains us, which we enjoy. At some point in time, the pattern seems to become restrictive, but in reality *we are the ones who have moved.* The pattern is stationary and static. While we have been using it for support, we have grown and changed, and so we no longer need this particular form of assistance. This is the time to acknowledge our growth and let go of what no longer serves us. In a spirit of celebration, we must see the ways in which our predicament is positive and good. Remember that negative judgment holds resistance and resentment in place, and when that happens we are stuck, stuck, stuck. To get unstuck, we need to acknowledge the value of the pattern, the good it has provided. Think of positive framing as Teflon and negative framing as glue. As we honor ourselves for our initial choice and our resultant progress, what no longer serves us is free to fall away. It's as if we pull the plug on the negative energy that fuels the old pattern, and so the pattern collapses. True recognition of how the pattern has been good for us, combined with positive recognition of our choices, accelerates our growth beyond our wildest dreams.

Interconnectedness: The Dance of Give and Take

There is another fascinating piece of this work that the Records show us. As we travel our soul's path, in this lifetime and others, we are not alone—our path is well populated. It may seem to us at times that we have taken on other people's ideas. We may even believe that they have forced their ideas upon us. It can certainly seem that way, but that is not really what is occurring. There is a human ocean blanketing the planet, connecting us all. Our interrelatedness is a fact of our existence, and it provides for the exchange of ideas, beliefs, feelings, attitudes, perceptions, and understandings. We take what we need from these exchanges. We adopt those perceptions that are right for us at the time. At the same time, we release and let go of what is no longer appropriate for us, discharging it into the pool of collective consciousness. There, whomever resonates with it is sure to find it.

This is the magnificent flow of human life. We take from others and they take from us. We give to others and they give to us. Everyone on the planet is engaged in this great exchange. All of us are actively involved whether we are consciously aware of our participation or not. It may seem at times like others are brainwashing us or stuffing their erroneous mythologies down our throats—or that we are doing the same to them. But this is an energetic impossibility. While the great exchange is under way, there is another powerful law at work, one you can explore in your Akashic Records.

The law in charge of interconnectedness is that we can only take what is ours, what fits us at the moment. We do not take on anyone else's beliefs unless they fit us and are appropriate for us at the time. We cannot be forced to do anything unless at some level we know that this is our very best option at the time, and we accept it. Yes, we may have lifetimes when we are victims persecuted beyond belief. It is also true that we have lifetimes in which we victimize others. But in order for us to take on the beliefs of another, we have to be in harmony with them; otherwise, the ideas will not stick to us. By the same token, we can bombard others with our seductive powers of persuasion, and it may appear that they have absorbed our ideas, but if our relationship is not a perfect fit, the glimmer will quickly dull and they will walk away. Others cannot hold us hostage and we cannot hold others hostage. And this is very good news for us all.

Having acquired the awareness that we can only adopt and absorb what is in harmony with who we are, we need never worry about being had, conned, or fooled. There is no reason to be overconcerned about coercing others. Remember that we are all individually responsible for our experience, interpretations, awareness, and consciousness, because we all have the same access to the power of life. This inner power is equally available to each and every one of us. This is the ultimate democracy of the spiritual realm.

So we now understand that we ourselves determine, consciously or unconsciously, whether a pattern is appropriate for us at any given time. At the same time, we are the ones who determine the ideal moment to release the pattern. No one else can take a pattern from us because we alone have authority over our Innermost Self: we are the lords of our own manors. Others may exert tremendous effort to cause us to change our patterns, but no one else has our strength of influence at the core level of our Being. By the same token, we can bribe others, threaten, ply with kindness, grate with guilt—oh, the possibilities are endless—but in the final analysis, it is not in our power, not in our sphere of influence, to cause another human being to change patterns. As you examine such efforts in the Records, you find that they are actually demeaning, degrading, and insulting. When we take on the task of changing another, with or without the intensity of religious fervor, we are in effect saying that we know what's right for her, more than she does. This is never correct. Part of becoming spiritually mature is becoming aware of and accepting the fact that each of us has the wholeness of Divine wisdom within—no exceptions.

Our challenge is to see the Light in others, to trust them with their own lives, to know the truth about who they are even when they themselves temporarily forget. And this brings us back to "Judge Not," one of the three Absolutes of the Records. As we see ourselves and others in the Light of the Akashic Records, we find that indeed we are all equal in that Light. We discover that there is nothing that truly warrants our judgment. All the choices people make are valid. There is no such thing as being "off path." All of life is the path, even detours into madness, fear, and indulgence of every kind. More accurately, we are the path, for it is through our very selves that we come to know the reality of the Divine Presence. In fact, we are the path along which we transform and carry ourselves through time, space, and experience. We can expand our awareness to appreciate that we are all in this together, we are all traveling companions, and we can trust that Life is unfolding through us, as us—even if we do not see evidence of this. Trust and know that we will let go of limiting patterns when the time is right.

Enslavement and Freedom

Both enslavement and freedom are characterized by patterns in our consciousness that we adopt with the intent to improve ourselves. These patterns of thinking, feeling, and behaving are chosen because we think they are the very best idea at the time we chose them. Supported by these structures, we eventually grow beyond them. This is the shift point in our relationship with these patterns—where we move from positive support into enslavement or freedom.

In the case of enslavement, we try to make an outdated habit work. When it does not work, then we judge ourselves negatively. This judgment acts like glue, holding the pattern in place; we are stuck with it. Until we make peace with ourselves, it is ours. As we begin to accept responsibility and recognize the ways in which this pattern has benefited us, the tensions of judgment and resistance dissolve—liberating us from the pattern!

The big difference between enslavement and freedom is our response. With freedom, we celebrate our accomplishment as we arrive at the supportive edge of a pattern. Honoring the pattern's positive value loosens the energetic hold it previously had, allowing us to release it and move on to the next best pattern we may choose.

Patterns themselves are neutral. It is our relationship to them that determines our enslavement or liberation. Negative judgments, resistance, and fear keep us stuck, whereas acceptance, appreciation, and benefit of the doubt guide us into greater states of freedom. Governed by the three Absolutes, "Judge Not," "Fear Not," and "Resist Not," the Akashic Records are an ideal atmosphere for facilitating the freedom we deserve.

❖

Our explorations so far have been focusing on the process of attaining freedom from limiting patterns: moving from enslavement to empowerment. We addressed our understanding of freedom itself. We discussed the life cycle of patterns, and explored the structure of both the pattern of enslavement and the pattern of empowerment. We learned some strategies for dissolving the scaffolding of undesirable patterns. Now, I invite you to take a look at some of these issues within your Records and observe them from the point of view of your Soul.

Our freedom from limiting patterns is fundamental to experiencing our relationships with others as a pathway to peace. It enables us to be in the world in a productive and satisfying way. Freedom is vital to our ability to engage with other people in authentic and powerful relationships, reducing obstacles that interfere with self-expression and the joy of living. We are each drops in a wider ocean of humanity. Therefore, our ability to live in harmony within ourselves while in the company of several billion people is essential. And beyond living in harmony lies the opportunity to join in humanity's odyssey, a communal experience. Our personal freedom ensures that we can do both: be our most authentic selves and engage in the world. Our work in the Akashic Records opens all the doorways through which we need to pass.

◆

Akashic Reflections

Open Your Records

- Bring to mind a pattern in your life that you are unhappy about.

- Ask your Masters, Teachers, and Loved Ones to help you see the point at which you chose this pattern.

- Explore how it was your best option at the time. Make note of how it has served you, when it fulfilled its original function, and how it has served you even beyond its original function.

- Find out from your Masters, Teachers, and Loved Ones what you need to do to let it go. If you are unclear about their suggestions, ask for clarity. Stay with it until you are reasonably sure that you can do what they recommend.

- As you work with this pattern in your Records and it begins to dissolve, celebrate your progress.

Close Your Records

Open Your Records

- Ask your Masters, Teachers, and Loved Ones to help you examine your relationship with freedom.

- What do you like about freedom? What do you *not* like about freedom?

- Where did you get the idea that it is good for you to be free?

- Where did you get the idea that it is good for you *not* to be too free?

- What or who will support you in being comfortable with your next level of freedom?

Close Your Records

Open Your Records

- Ask your Masters, Teachers, and Loved Ones to help you see times when you forced your own ideas on others.

- Ask them to show you times when you enslaved others and why you believed this to be a good idea. Remember that there are countless gradations of enslavement.

- Ask them to show you times when you adopted the limiting ideas of others. Why was that a fine idea at the time?

- Ask them to help you investigate times when you were enslaved by others and how you were served by that experience.

Close Your Records

Open Your Records

- Ask your Masters, Teachers, and Loved Ones to help you see times when you encouraged freedom in others.

- Ask them to help you discover times when you went out of your way to encourage freedom in others.

- Ask them to show you times when others encouraged you to be freer than ever before.

- Ask them to help you see times when others went out of their way to encourage your freedom.

- Request that your Masters, Teachers, and Loved Ones help you prepare for the next step in the expansion of your freedom.

Close Your Records

Our Sacred Wounds as a Platform for Transcendence and Transformation in the World: Working with the Ascension Matrix

PART FOUR

✦

Introduction

We have now traveled through the first two stages of healing through the Akashic Records. We have explored our Sacred Wounds as points of power in relationship with ourselves. We have crossed the bridge that connects us with others, shifting into an awareness of our Sacred Wounds as a pathway of peace. And so now we arrive at a new shore, one that promises the most profound change of all.

Here we find the Promised Land, the land of freedom from our past and freedom to embrace our future in a new world. Like the great explorers of our planet centuries ago, we too are voyagers—of the interior terrain. Having arrived at the edge of our own frontier, we are now free to venture forth in peace and with enthusiasm to discover the best of who we are and what life has to offer us.

This remarkable stage of our healing journey involves investigating our Sacred Wounds as the platform for transcendence and transformation in the world. We are in the final stretch, standing in the clearing of new possibilities. Here, facing our wounds catapults us into a new way of living. We begin to know what it means to be "in the world, but not of it." Our newfound access to inner power makes it possible for us to both transcend and transform while being fully engaged in the world.

When we speak of transcendence in this context, we refer to rising above or going beyond our human limitations without condemnation. If it is indeed best for us to do so, we can surpass them. At the same time, we transform. Through our work in the Akashic Records at this level, we are truly changed.

Before we proceed further, let us list and appreciate our accomplishments. By now our relationship with our wounds has been radically altered. Wounds that had previously been obstructions to the realization of the perfection of our soul have become gateways to a direct experience of our goodness. Wounds that had dimmed our awareness of the Innermost Self have become points of power in our relationship with our self. By daring to walk through the darkness of our pain and the unknown, we have found the Light within; it has always been there, but only now can we live in its radiance. Our need to abandon and reject ourselves has been relieved and replaced by the regular practice of unconditional self-love. This practice enables us to relax, and as we do so, we discover that we can be the person we have always known we are at our core. The Innermost Self now has the means to come forward, and this brings a remarkable level of satisfaction and pleasure to us and to everyone we meet.

After establishing a rewarding relationship with ourselves, we turned to the difficulties we had in our connections with other people. We discovered that the resentments blocking our path are actually opportunities for revealing new levels of love and harmony within ourselves and between us. Surprisingly, we have found that the patterns of restriction and limitation that held us hostage are actually pathways into an awe-inspiring dimension of freedom that has become our new home. Here, we drop anchor and settle in to live a new life.

The questions that fuel our progress now are "How can I contribute? How can I serve? What can I bring? How can I be helpful?" In our final step of healing through the Akashic Records, we will look at how we can live an Ascending Life. Now that the healing has begun, we want to consider how we can keep growing, developing, and enjoying. We no longer have to live lives focused upon strategically avoiding pain and suffering—those days are over. Now our challenge is learning how to expand our ability to love and be loved. This is our time to explore the joy of living! We are now moving toward the Light, being led by the Light within, hearing the call of the Light.

There will be times when we have to go back to basics and renew the intensity of the practices we have learned so far, but that is to be expected: we are still human and we can expect to hit some speed bumps. But the general climate of our lives is different. We have a new ground of being; we are anchored in and aware of the Light. If we encounter a painful problem, we can use it to propel ourselves forward and upward into the Light, rather than using it as a weapon against ourselves. In the promised land of freedom, the question driving our quest becomes "How much love and happiness am I willing to enjoy?"

Living an Ascending Life

Having cleaned house, we have become clearer channels of Light, ready to explore living an Ascending Life beyond our woundedness. In this section we will examine the idea of Ascension and get acquainted with an exciting new construct that was revealed to me over time within the Akashic Records: the Ascension Matrix. In the next few short chapters, we will consider each component of the Matrix to see how it functions independently of, and interdependently with, its Matrix mates. We will explore what it means for us to live as Ascending Beings and how to do this in our everyday lives.

Ascension can be defined as conscious fusion with the Divine. The truth is that we are already and always one with Divine Life. However, we are not always aware of this Truth. One of the most significant steps we will ever take in the evolution of our consciousness is the step from being oblivious to our fusion with the Divine to being keenly aware of it. Our consciousness of this fusion allows us to naturally transcend—rise above our mortal existence—and live in a dimension of unlimited possibilities.

Ascension itself is the consequence of inner alignment. We do not directly cause our Ascension through force of will: focusing on the act itself will not do the job. However, we can activate it by using our Sacred Wounds to tap into Divine Power as a path of peace and alignment. When we do this, our Ascension is assured.

Ascension is not a one-time event—we do not rise once and forever. It is very much alive as an ongoing state or condition. As infinite beings, we have the potential for infinite Ascension—an unlimited ability to rise above and go beyond our human condition, buoyed by the ever-expanding, ever-deepening awareness that we are one with the Divine Presence.

Fusion itself is a fascinating process in which substances are brought together, blended, and transformed into a state of union. When particles of varying weights fuse, there is a tremendous release of energy. In the fusion associated with Ascension, our relatively dense human selves join with a significantly lighter Divine Spirit—and profound energy is generated. Many of us who work in the Records are familiar with the manifestation of this in everyday life. Stepping onto the spiritual path consciously, we enter into new levels of awareness, new dimensions of knowing, and experience new sensitivities. Realms of previously unrecognized possibilities are seen, and as this happens, we have access to expanded states of energy. It is common to feel hyper-alive, über-alert, wide awake.

When in this state, you find yourself living a "quickened" life, one that accelerates and brings increased clarity. You can see where you are going, and you can see beyond appearances into what is truly driving the events in your life. Your perceptions are heightened and you have tremendous vitality, which is released by the fusion process. This vital force propels you forward; it urges you into life. One of the most compelling aspects of present-day spirituality is that the powerful force released in the fusion process enables you to move into life, fully conscious of your spiritual nature and engaged as an authentic human being.

Our awareness of what is happening gives us greater authority over our direction. Awareness, by its nature, amplifies the energy coursing through us—it fortifies the force and supercharges us. We can channel increasing awareness and energy into those things that uplift and edify us. Without this awareness, we may enjoy the experience but lack authority over the process. It's as if we're taking this trip in the passenger seat instead of driving. Our journey may be delightful but incomplete. We will lack firsthand knowledge of the terrain, the route, the pitfalls, and the elegant stretches of the journey, as we will not fully comprehend the adventure.

When energy is released in this fusion process, it can seem like a big bang, an explosion that hurls us out of our current level of consciousness into a higher one. This can seem instantaneous—as though we suddenly took a flying leap. If we look deeper, we see that the energy is indeed propelling us outward and upward. But if we could observe the action in slow motion and chart it on a graph, we would see something different: a series of small, manageable steps, one following another. The incline would be steep, comprised of a series of tiny segments. We have constructed an internal scaffolding enabling our rise to the next level of consciousness.

The Ascension Matrix

This fusion process is what we experience in Ascension. With this understanding in place, we can address the Ascension Matrix, the subject of the next part of our journey.

As I said earlier, focusing on Ascending does not cause lift-off. What will activate the Ascension experience is our conscious engagement with the dynamics of the Ascension Matrix, established by a mixture of three qualities: Gratitude, Grace, and Generosity. Placing our attention on these components and creating further inner alignment will activate the Matrix, so our Ascent can commence. The phenomenon of Ascension is part of the whole of creation—it is already in place, and we do not have to cause it to exist. Our part is to establish right relations with our Sacred Wounds, align with creation, and focus on the qualities of the Matrix, for this is where we have maximum impact.

Each of the three dimensions of the Matrix makes its own contribution to the dynamics of the whole. The first component is Gratitude, which supplies *momentum*. The second is Grace, the *catalyst* for the matrix. Generosity is the final piece, and it provides *buoyancy,* making it easy to rise to the next level. Through the combination of these qualities, the Matrix operates to facilitate our progression from one higher level to the next, from one expanded state to another even greater expansion, from glory to glory to glory.

CHAPTER TEN

Gratitude

Gratitude is the first component of the Ascension Matrix—it propels us forward by creating momentum. Here on the Earth plane, it is important to move ahead with both feet on the ground; momentum enables us to do so at a steady pace. Gratitude—the state of thankfulness—is what creates these conditions. When we are grateful, we can recognize the positive value of the people and things around us and appreciate them. Gratitude is widely accepted as a potent antidote to depression, gloomy attitudes, and moods; it is an essential ingredient for sound mental health. It is a deceptively simple idea, but not so easy to accomplish. As has been the case throughout this healing process, this aspect is also best approached as a spiritual practice.

Feeling Gratitude for who we are, where we are, and what we have helps us break through our current level. As a starting point, we remain open to the possibility that what is present in our current reality has come into existence because it can benefit us in some way. Willingness to acknowledge this is essential to activate the state of Gratitude. It's easy and quite natural to be thankful when we get what we want or when things go our way. It is another matter altogether when it seems like we will never realize our dreams, our hearts have been broken, we lose something or someone we love, or we fail to achieve a goal. Yet, it is possible to achieve Gratitude under these conditions, to open to thankfulness even when we are baffled by what is going on. It requires open-mindedness; it does not require understanding. The mere willingness to be grateful collapses the resistance wedged between our Innermost Self and the life force, and this creates an opening through which the Light can seep in and our pain can drain away.

Gratitude is the result of a choice, an act of will. Once we decide to consider the option of being grateful no matter what transpires, we place ourselves in a position to receive all the good that can possibly come from a situation. The more we are open to goodness without prescribing exactly how it is to be delivered to us, the more of it we will receive. Even when we are tangled up in disaster and dismay, the moment we muster the willingness to be grateful, we align with all the positive possibilities inherent in these circumstances. At first, it is surprising to discover that the most distressing situation has positivity woven through it, but over time we realize that Gratitude is always present; we need only receive.

The energy of Gratitude gathers, collects, and accelerates. This has a cumulative effect: momentum compounds. This effect assists us in breaking through our current level to the next best location in consciousness. The momentum-gathering action of Gratitude enables us to reach a state known as "escape velocity," which is the rate of speed necessary for something to move beyond the influence of gravity. It can also be thought of as the speed required to break through our current level of consciousness. Gratitude gives us the energy we need to move past the gravity of the zone we currently occupy. Because Gratitude gathers, fills, and holds more and more energy, it continually strengthens, supporting us in moving through our internal limitations and restrictions toward our next level of awareness.

Even when we are residing in a good place, there is always another, even better place: this is the nature of ongoing Ascension. There is wonderful and there is more wonderful and, yes, there is even more wonderful. As infinite beings in an infinite universe, we have access to infinite states of goodness in a variety of expressions. The only restriction that exists is our ability to accept infinite goodness. As we grow into increased happiness, health, love, fun, and the joy of living, it can be hard to accept that there is even more available to us. This is the opportunity of the Ascending Life: to remain in Gratitude to fuel our escape velocity, and to remain open to an ongoing experience of greater goodness.

Experiencing gratitude requires a conscious choice. It is not accidental, nor is it bestowed upon us by some mysterious force. Deliberately moving toward this state of being is the right use of your will. Of course, you want to draw upon all the energetic support available to you. In the final analysis, *you* are responsible for entering into a state of Gratitude. Fortunately, your current location is always the perfect starting place.

Begin by returning to a central premise of healing through the Akashic Records. Consider that your whole life is a conspiracy on the part of the physical world to demonstrate to you that you are lovable, that everyone around you is helping you to realize your goodness, and that every event—from the mundane details of your day to international affairs—is orchestrated to wake you up to the ever-present Light. *Pretend* that you are grateful for everything if that's all you can manage now, and start to take note. Ask yourself, "If I were grateful, what would I be grateful for?" Although the issue is quite serious, it is acceptable to play with the question while knowing that at some time in your soul's journey you will choose to be grateful for everything. You may make that decision today or you may wait twenty years or another thirty-seven lifetimes. It's all right; you will do this at the perfect time. You are completely committed to knowing your own Soul and its perfection, so relax. You can count on yourself.

Gratitude is a natural part of your innermost Being. It is in your Soul's DNA. You have within you a consciousness of Gratitude that does not depend on anything outside of yourself. It does not rely upon getting what you want, meeting certain goals, or anyone else behaving in a certain manner. It is part of your basic makeup as a person. Your growth and your expansion into higher realms are embedded into the code of your soul. The path is within you and reveals itself to you as you become ready, willing, and able to proceed.

Let me sum up this discussion of Gratitude. To move forward in your life, direct your attention to Gratitude and then let it take the reins. There is no need to push yourself ahead or force your circumstances—that won't work over the long haul anyway. Focus on being thankful and sincere, and you will travel into the heart of ever-expanding goodness.

◆

Akashic Reflections

Open Your Records

- Ask your Masters, Teachers, and Loved Ones to reveal to you how you would benefit from developing an attitude of Gratitude for all things.

- Ask them to help you see how you can attain that state of being.

Close Your Records

Open Your Records

- Ask your Masters, Teachers, and Loved Ones to enable you to recognize how your personal experience of Gratitude would impact the circumstances of your everyday life.

Close Your Records

Open Your Records

- Ask your Masters, Teachers, and Loved Ones to assist you in seeing how being thankful supports your escape velocity and your ability to move to the next level of consciousness.

Close Your Records

Open Your Records

- Request that your Masters, Teachers, and Loved Ones help you to locate that part of yourself that is eternally grateful.

Close Your Records

◆

Homework

I invite you to practice being thankful for the reality of who you are and for your life, just the way it is. There are bound to be things about your life that you do not like, but allow yourself to be grateful for them anyway. Just consider the possibility that everything occurring in your world is designed to bring more good your way, to support your awareness of your own Divine nature and the Divine nature of everyone else. Practicing Gratitude is simple: say "Thank you" to everyone and everything. The results may astonish you. Enjoy the ride!

CHAPTER ELEVEN

Grace

The second element in our Ascension Matrix is Grace. Grace functions as the catalyst for our next leap in consciousness. In this section, we will take a closer look at the Matrix itself to understand how it operates within us. We will explore the properties of Grace and its role in the Matrix. Then we will investigate our personal relationship with, and responsibility to, Grace as well as some of the more obvious expressions of Grace in our lives. This is a very exciting part of our work together because we are closing in on the precise point of power in our Matrix.

Let's first define "matrix." A matrix is a situation or condition within which something new originates or develops. In our case, this "something new" comes about as a result of the relationship among three distinct categories of energy: Grace, Gratitude, and Generosity.

In the Ascension Matrix, Grace is the catalyst and Gratitude and Generosity are additional, cooperative, active ingredients. If we were baking bread, Grace would be the yeast in the recipe, causing the other ingredients to interact in a way that would not occur without it. However, all three are required to form the Matrix; it is their unique *interaction* that is required to provide for the origin of something new. In our case, the something new is transcendence—rising above our current level of awareness—in the form of Ascension, or conscious fusion with the Divine.

Grace occupies the center of the Matrix. It behaves as any catalyst does: it either initiates or accelerates a reaction without being affected itself. Grace can generate or speed up a change in the properties of its two cooperative partners, yet it remains true to its own composition. It has a remarkably stabilizing effect. When Grace is added to Gratitude and Generosity, both are enhanced, and the three come together to establish a new situation. The goal as these three energies interact is to go beyond our current level of consciousness, transform our relationship with life, and operate in the dimension of freedom from the dictates of the past.

By itself, Grace is the disposition to be helpful or generous. It is mercy and goodwill. Most commonly, we recognize these as religious ideas because they have been a topic of discussion in religious circles for centuries. Grace is understood as an aspect of Divine love and protection that has been bestowed upon humanity out of the goodness of Divine nature itself. It is a state of being protected or sanctified by God's goodwill, and also a power or energy force granted by God. Clearly, this religious understanding is in some ways helpful and is certainly familiar to most Westerners. A limitation of the religious slant, however, is the notion that we do not deserve Grace. From the perspective of the Akashic Records, this idea does not make sense. In the Records, we learn that we can only experience what is resonant with our own consciousness. We recognize Grace because it is an essential element of who we are.

As with Divine nature itself, the determining factor in connecting to Grace is our level of awareness. Grace is always everywhere, present and available to us. If we are awake to this idea, we can access it. If we are asleep to the presence of Grace, we do not have access to it—it's that simple. As our awareness increases and we become more familiar with its presence, it may seem that Grace itself is expanding. In reality, when we detect Grace, we are only becoming aware of what has always existed.

Our ideas of the Divine and its nature are critical when it comes to availing ourselves of Grace. If we have a perception of the Divine as compassionate and generous, we will have more access to Grace than if we think the Divine Presence is stingy or mean-spirited. Our understanding of Divine authority determines our access to its resources. We are able to grasp and experience the benefits of Grace as long as we recognize the *reality* of it. Again, we are dealing with an infinite, eternal energy. Wherever we are now in our level of awareness, there is always more for us. This is a process with which we can engage for eternity.

We have a role to play in our relationship to Grace, a responsibility even: to allow Grace to do what it does best, to be its authentic self. The great possibility inherent in our conscious awareness of Grace is to release unnecessary effort and striving, because within Grace, the Light does all the work. We can quit laboring, relying on our efforts to bring about our heart's desires. Once we touch into our awareness of Grace, we can lay down our tools. Our new position is to be *beholders* of Grace. As we recognize and observe the presence of Grace, we expand our awareness of it, and our expanding awareness enhances our ability to receive, draw upon, and absorb its qualities. It may appear to us that Grace is becoming a stronger influence in our lives, but in reality, it has always been potent—we are simply waking up to this fact.

As beholders of Grace, there is very little we need to do. We have no need to try to manage it, no reason to attempt to activate or deactivate any process or state. We can merely detect and identify Grace where we encounter it and allow for the reality that we are in the presence of a profound quality of love and wisdom. This is the most natural thing in the world: to observe with reverence this presence that has been with us throughout time.

Once we give ourselves the chance to sit in the presence of Grace, we will notice more about its qualities and characteristics. We will be able to discern that it is expansive by nature: it seems to move outward from its own center point, its deepest core. What is obviously missing is any intrinsic container for this exquisite energy. Grace requires a space through which it can flow and expand and in which it can be held; we humans are that space.

Another distinct quality of Grace is that it is of the moment, very much in the present. There is no saving it up or stockpiling it for an emergency; it is always fresh and immediate. At the same time, it is *all* available in the now. The allness of Grace is ours, one moment at a time, compelling us to a new level of authentic presence to the wholeness of creation.

Much as with Gratitude, there is a location, a dimension within each and every one of us that is Grace itself. Were it not within us, we would never recognize it beyond ourselves. Somewhere inside you there is an infinite well of Grace that is yours, for now and always, as you become open to the possibility and then the probability of its presence within you. You may want to experiment with Grace: go within and call out for guidance to be led to that part of your Innermost Self where you can settle in and relish the experience of beholding Grace. One of the ways you will know that more Grace than ever before is moving through you is a sense of the presence of goodness, which is an expression of Grace. Feeling good is the clue that you are on the right track. The sense of goodness—that there is a rightness at work no matter what is happening—is the doorway to this dimension. The sense that all is well is the big hint, the clue. Follow it.

The way to truly know that you are in the flow of Grace more than ever before is to evaluate your emotional resilience. Sensational phenomena—a flush of warmth, a buzzing at the crown of the head—may occur, but they are not reliable indicators of progress; they can be fascinating and fun but distracting, making us miss the point of our spiritual progress.

The point is to become free of limiting patterns, resentments, and other forms of self-centered fears, and move toward more actively loving ourselves and others. As people, we want to look for signs that we are becoming more understanding, more compassionate, more patient, more kind, less worried, and happier than ever before. If these qualities are developing, we know Grace is at work.

As you pay close attention to the presence of Grace, your relationship to it, and its impact on you, you will be able to discern how its energy affects the whole of the Matrix. You will see how it operates as a catalyst. Grace quickens the process of Gratitude, thereby accelerating momentum. Feeling Gratitude is easy and completely natural in the presence of Grace. At the same time, Grace triggers Generosity, which provides lift-off in our Matrix. We will look at Generosity in greater depth in the next chapter. For now, just know that the act of giving enables you to lighten up and rise to new heights.

Notice how the three qualities work together within you. The Ascension Matrix is alive within the Innermost Self. It has always been a part of you, simply waiting for activation. Your willingness to be grateful—for both what is and what is not in your life—and your openness to new levels of Generosity fuel the Matrix. With your developing awareness of Grace, you are on your way to transcending your present state and living beyond your old ideas.

Perhaps you will discern the moment of lift-off when you travel from one level of consciousness to another, and you will perceive the interaction within the Matrix propelling you forward. Grace has activated the Matrix. Gratitude has gathered the power sufficient to establish the escape velocity you need to break through your current boundaries. Generosity has liberated you from the burden of inappropriate withholding. Together, they have served to aid your transcendence from your ordinary state of consciousness into extraordinary realms governed by your conscious awareness of Oneness with Divine Light.

♦

Akashic Reflections

Open Your Records

- Ask your Masters, Teachers, and Loved Ones to provide you with a direct experience of Grace.

Close Your Records

Open Your Records

- Request the help of your Masters, Teachers, and Loved Ones to locate the infinite reservoir of Grace within you.

Close Your Records

Open Your Records

- Ask your Masters, Teachers, and Loved Ones to guide you through the operation of the Ascension Matrix, with Grace as a catalyst.

Close Your Records

Open Your Records

- Ask your Masters, Teachers, and Loved Ones to enable you to recognize how you can expand your awareness of Grace.

Close Your Records

Open Your Records

- Ask your Masters, Teachers, and Loved Ones to assist you in learning how your awareness of Grace can transform a current life challenge you are facing.

Close Your Records

◆

Homework

Behold the ever-present reality of Grace within you, beyond you, and through you. Enjoy!

CHAPTER TWELVE

Generosity

We turn now to the final piece of the Ascension Matrix: Generosity, which lends buoyancy to the Matrix. Generosity works by fostering giving and enabling us to lighten up. As we become less dense, we find it easier to move to a new level of consciousness. Generosity promotes our ability to move upward and outward simultaneously. This is vital to our Ascension experience, which by its nature involves moving both above and beyond our current level of consciousness. As we give, we let go—we release and become more buoyant. No longer retaining or holding on, we gracefully ascend and transcend, and our relationship with the world is transformed.

Generosity is the spirit of giving. Expansive in nature, Generosity moves through the heart. It involves being ready and willing to give, to extend, to reach out. There is no stinginess, no hoarding, no withholding—no anorexia of the spirit. Generosity is about opening up and letting the life force move from the deepest regions of the Innermost Self, through your heart, and out into life. It can feel like a breaking open or a breaking free. As the pulse of life moves through the heart, the heart is transfigured. Hard-heartedness dissolves, frost thaws, and tight pathways open. Wherever we are on the continuum of Generosity, whether our hearts are shut down or wide open and free—the act of giving transforms us—we can progress to our next step.

Giving is natural; it is the basis of our constitution. We see this even in our breathing patterns. As we exhale, we are giving. Every exhale is followed by an inhale, corresponding to receiving. What initiates this rhythm is giving; it always precedes receiving. As we give, we make more room within to receive. We cannot receive if we are full to the brim.

As we initiate the rhythmic pattern of giving and receiving, we enter into a transformational relationship with the flow of life. Notice how giving affects your sense of gravity, your boundedness to the Earth. It lightens you. You feel freer, less burdened. It's as if you've been hovering, barely airborne, in a hot air balloon. With each act of giving, you release one of the many sandbags that keep you from soaring. Actual giving makes the difference.

Originally, the idea of Generosity was tied to nobility—high social rank or status in society—and in its application here, this makes a great deal of sense. To be generous, we must experience ourselves to be of noble lineage: in this case spiritual lineage, our sacred roots. We must know ourselves to be people with something to offer, people who have more than enough of something of value. The offered item can be any number of things: money, kindness, a good sense of humor. As we recognize that we have something to share and are willing to give, we enter into a dimension of consciousness very similar to those who consider themselves nobility—we have a sense of entitlement that is true and positive.

Equality is one of the values of our age: we like to think that we are all equal and have access to the same resources. In so many ways, though, this is not true. We do not all have the same athletic talent, financial resources, mathematical ability, or social acumen. What is exactly the same for each and every one of us, however, is that we have the same oneness with Life; we all have the same spiritual connection, the same essential relationship with the Divine. We do not all have the same awareness of it, but we are all direct descendants of the Divine, part of a flow of life that is infinite and eternal. This is our shared noble ancestry, our spiritual lineage. The greater our awareness of this, the easier it is to give, and give freely.

As we become able to comprehend ourselves as people who have something to offer in any given moment, we need to touch back again on judgment, because we want to be clear about what enables us to actually step forward and make our contributions. There are two sides of judgment, that of self and that of others. If we have negative perceptions about others who seem to know they have much to give, if we doubt the motives of those who are very generous with their resources, if we think others aren't giving proportionate to their ample means, we are setting ourselves up for paralysis. We will not be able to be generous if we have negative judgments about other givers—why would we let ourselves be included in a group that has not merited our approval? Perhaps we think people who give are foolish, or that they're pushovers. The possibilities for condemnation are many. Our opportunity is to exercise the absolute "Judge Not."

It is helpful to instead consider that it is good to give, that sharing is a positive act, that others benefit from giving—that they may even be transformed by their giving. As we cultivate an understanding of these beneficial effects, we will find Generosity appealing, enticing us to take action in that direction.

Inner and Outer Aspects of Generosity

As we observe continually in the Akashic Records, just as with everything else present on this Earth, Generosity has both inner and outer aspects. Physical, material life is an expression of internal, invisible consciousness. As we explore our inner terrain, our Earthly life adjusts to reflect our evolving awareness. This is occurring both at the level of the individual and the whole of humanity. All progress—exploring outer space, increasing knowledge in science and medicine, developing instantaneous communication, and other advancements—is representative of our expanding conscious awareness. Even our understanding that the Earth is round was a natural result of our expanding inner awareness. During our time, as we are realizing our oneness with everyone on the planet and all life, we see old national identities begin to dissolve and technologies that support global communication emerge. This transition enables us to live our everyday lives from the truth of our oneness with "All That Is."

When it comes to Generosity, our ideal is that our external, active giving is a direct expression of our internal values. Our entire healing process supports the collapse of the gap between our Innermost Self and expression into Life. In the Ascension phase of our progression, we are positioned to transform our expression in the world around us, and one dimension of this is to let Generosity flow from our inner world to the outer.

As I mentioned earlier, giving always requires action in the world. And truly, very few of us are called to a life of silent reflection and prayer, particularly at this time in history. This is a time to act, to work in the world. When this action is a direct expression of our truth and values, the giving itself is satisfying, no matter how the recipient responds. We can call this authentic giving. When we give from our Innermost Self, our gift is always well received. The beneficiary experiences not only the action or the material object, but the accompanying energy. Fascinating!

When there is a disconnect between our Innermost Self and the action we take, giving is rarely satisfying, and we can call this disconnected giving. The experience is frustrating as we are often misunderstood by the recipient. Our original intention and primary focus can be diluted or even lost in the process. The recipient is then presented with an action corrupted by confusing emotional energy, or a material object with an absence of energy, a hollowness. This is what happens when we receive a gift that does not feel right to us, that maybe even seems inappropriate. It's an indication that the giver and the recipient are disconnected in a similar way, as we would not be engaged with someone who is not in harmony with our inner state. The situation presents us with an opportunity to wake up and examine where we may have a similar challenge. Once we have resolved this, our giving to and receiving from others adjusts to reflect our new level of inner awareness.

Giving with an Agenda

All too often, giving is used as a bargaining chip—we give to get something in return. This is always a recipe for disaster; it is not a good idea, and it doesn't work. Giving conditionally in this way is an insulting form of control. We give because it makes us feel superior to others and because we think we know their destinies better than they do. This type of giving becomes a way to accumulate power over people, which is no use in developing relationships with dignity. We also want to be careful that our actions on others' behalf are not based on feeling sorry for them. Pity is not supportive; it suggests that we do not believe others have the same life force available to them, that we have more and are superior as a result.

Visible, Invisible, and Blended Gifts

The Records teach us that there are three kinds of authentic gifts: the visible, invisible, and a blend of the two. Energies or characteristics such as love and kindness and qualities like patience, respect, and sensitivity are in the invisible group. Visible gifts are physical or have material outcomes; they can be presents wrapped in a bow, financial support, or an action such as helping with any kind of task: cooking, babysitting, or building a house. Then there's a third category of gifts that combines both, the gift of time spent with someone simply for its own sake: companionship, support, engagement. There may not be a particular task involved, but there is a blend of the energy of presence and the action of being physically available.

There is a continuum of giving. On one end, we give energy, positive feelings, and qualities such as kindness and respect. At the other end of the spectrum are tangibles, actions, and necessary things. When we are consciously connected to our Innermost Self and allow our most precious inner resources to move out from that place into life, we will find ourselves giving a blend of both; this is optimal giving where we are able to extend the best of who we are to others. We are compassionate, supportive, understanding; we easily find ways to act in accordance with those traits; and we are able to locate needed material things that represent the condition of our consciousness. It becomes second nature to notice the needs of others as opportunities to be supportive and take generous action.

Withholding ceases to be an option. It doesn't feel good to hold back love, support, kindness, or the material things we have or can do that would be beneficial to another. Through our work in the Records, we learn that it is impossible to give too much. If you feel you are giving too much, this is a signal that you are not giving what the other really needs, that you are not giving from the deepest part of yourself, or that the thing (time, money, stuff, active assistance) you are giving is not the best expression of your true desire to share. Dig deeper, go within, ask what others need, and then give courageously and completely.

On Giving and Receiving

It may seem that we are a bit out of balance, focused on unbridled giving with little attention to receiving, but the wisdom of the Records tells us otherwise. This is where the whole of the Ascension Matrix becomes important. Considering the three components—Gratitude, Grace, and Generosity—we see that there is an active, cyclic relationship. As interaction among them takes place, there is a harmony of giving and receiving, receiving and giving, that will enable transformation in our relationships and with everyday living in the world. Any one of these parts on its own is valuable, but if we concentrate on one and exclude the others, we create imbalance in our lives. Together, Gratitude, Grace, and Generosity produce a condition of transcendence in which we can live as responsible, happy contributors, experiencing the blessings of our human experience.

Giving and receiving are actually two sides of the same coin. As we give, we have more room to receive. As we receive, we have more to give. Awareness of what we have to give is cultivated through the practices of both Gratitude and Generosity, which then amplify what we have to give and receive. The cycle is beautiful to behold.

Continuous giving enables us to maintain this ongoing transformation. If you have been a taker and you shift toward being a giver, you have found the best possible insurance policy for greater well-being. Move from giving a little to giving the best of who you are catapults you into the dimension of radical love and freedom. This will happen moment by moment. As with Grace, generous giving occurs in the now. The question that will fuel your journey from being stuck to experiencing liberation and joy is "What can I give *now?*"

We want to enter into this dance of giving and receiving whenever we can. Ideally, we do not judge where we are on the continuum; we just jump in wherever we can. If you find that being generous is not helpful at the moment, try being grateful for what you have. Or, ask to become aware of the presence of Grace. Take any opening; they all work together.

Let's be realistic about this flow of giving and receiving, especially about reciprocity. It is unusual to receive from those to whom we give. Our relationship with children illustrates this point well. It is unreasonable for an adult to expect an even return on what he or she gives to a child; the flow in this situation is naturally from adult to child. At some point, the child will certainly be capable of giving talents, time, and gifts to others. This is all part of the cycle, which is constantly moving. We simply need to be in the flow, giving and receiving, knowing that each role is vital. Everyone has something to give, and everyone has the capacity to receive; from the standpoint of the Akashic Records, the specifics of who receives what from whom are unimportant. It is by engaging in the actions of giving and receiving that we discover the value of our participation in life, who we are, what we have to offer, and how to appreciate the blessings of our existence.

Ultimately, we give because we are compelled to do so. An obvious quality of spiritually mature people is that they are generous. They share what they have and are helpful most of the time. They trust that they will get what they need, and they look out for the well-being of those they love. Their giving dignifies others. Look for these qualities of Light in yourself and others: goodness, kindness, compassion, patience, understanding, joy, and generosity. When you have a sense of the Light within you, you simply cannot resist your urge to give. Focus your attention and your intention on the Matrix, and you will inevitably become the amazing person you have always hoped to be.

I will conclude our discussion of Generosity with a final point. The "nowness" of Grace supports our ability to identify appropriate giving. Grace enables us to discern our patterns of giving, illuminating the nurturing consequences of true giving and the exhaustion that results from giving what we do not really have to someone who does not really want it. Grace guides us in knowing what is honorable and true in the moment.

Akashic Reflections

Open Your Records

- Ask of your Masters, Teachers, and Loved Ones, "What are the possibilities for my personal transformation through giving?"

Close Your Records

Open Your Records

- Ask your Masters, Teachers, and Loved Ones to show you how you can open yourself to receive more easily.

- Watch what happens as you receive more. How does this impact your relationships with others? How does this affect your participation in the world?

- What happens to your sense of personal well-being as you receive more? Ask your Masters, Teachers, and Loved Ones to illustrate for you how receiving activates your willingness and ability to give.

- Ask them to support you in recognizing what becomes possible when you receive what others have to offer: what is both possible for you and possible for your relationships.

Close Your Records

Open Your Records

- Join your Masters, Teachers, and Loved Ones and inquire about how generous acts truly make you lighter. Some provide a powerful surge in buoyancy, while others offer less. Ask your Masters, Teachers, and Loved Ones to help identify what will give you the most powerful lift. Find out what has a lesser impact. Notice what you are ready, willing, and able to give in your life today, and then give it.

Close Your Records

Open Your Records

- Ask your Masters, Teachers, and Loved Ones to help you become more comfortable with that sense of freedom—that uplifting, soaring feeling—that results from your generosity.

- Ask them to support you in recognizing others who share your level of Generosity.

Close Your Records

◆

Homework

Look within now, in this moment, and see what you can give, both in qualities and actions. Then, go ahead—give! After you have given, you will find yourself in a new moment. Look and see what you can give now. Give. Come back to this homework again and again. Find what you have to offer and give it. Feel your life becoming lighter, less burdensome. Enjoy!

CHAPTER THIRTEEN

Engaging the Ascension Matrix

Somewhere inside, you have always known that your life can be joyous and your contribution to your world significant. The Ascension Matrix offers a proven mechanism for you to realize the hopes and dreams you've held inside. It will provide you with a strategy to make a difference for yourself for the good of all.

Whenever you feel disconnected from the joy of living, whenever you feel stuck or powerless, pause for a moment and activate your Matrix. You can do this within your Records or outside of them—it works under either condition. Remember that you have three ways to set the Matrix in motion. Ask for help in knowing which of the three to contact first.

Gratitude, the Matrix's source of momentum, is a great place to start. Ask yourself, "If I felt grateful, what would I be grateful for?" It only takes a bit of Gratitude to activate your Matrix. Think of your family and your friends. What is one characteristic of a family member you appreciate? Take a deep breath, and feel yourself standing solidly on the floor. What is there about your body that you can be thankful for? Scan the room you're in and note any objects you appreciate because they are useful or beautiful. Look out your window, or better still, take a walk. Are there birds singing, breezes wafting? Are there children riding tricycles, or playing in the snow? What is there in your environment that could delight you if you gave it a chance? Turn your attention toward it, whether it's a small detail you can take note of or something so pleasing it makes you smile. Be thankful for your experience—a lot or a little—and you will set the Matrix humming.

If it seems that the experience of Gratitude is beyond reach just now, move on to Generosity, which gives buoyancy to the Matrix. You can always find a way to give. Ask yourself, "What can I give now?" Don't be too concerned with what it is or how much. Just give whatever you can in this moment. Would a friend like to hear from you on the phone? Would your son or daughter like to go to the park? Would a spouse enjoy an encouraging email? Can you donate a few dollars to a cause you care about? Do you know someone who would appreciate a bouquet of flowers? Giving anything at all—time, money, material items—will lift you up and kick-start the Matrix.

Sometimes in the midst of difficulty, you can register a sense of Grace—the catalyst of the Matrix. It might be just a faint inkling that something has arrived in your life to assist you—a presence or a force. Perhaps a strong sense of a powerful and benevolent energy sweeps through you, taking you by surprise.

You will know it when you see and feel it. Behold Grace and know that the Matrix is fully engaged.

Any one of these three qualities will activate your Ascension Matrix. Direct your focus to one of them and see where it takes you. Go with it. As you do, you are sure to move beyond and rise above the entanglements you face. You will find yourself participating and not being burdened. You will be free to take any action that makes you happy, and as you do, your very happiness itself will be a blessing to everyone around you.

From the new altitude attained, observe yourself, your everyday life, your community, and your world. What contribution can you make that would thrill and inspire you? Now, free of complications, you will more clearly see what you can do to make the difference you have been hoping for in your world.

Understanding that the Ascension Matrix is there for you, and knowing how to use it, you become the generous giver you naturally are. You bring forth your powerful ideas for making your world, your home, better than before. As one of the soul group of humans on the Earth at this time who knows that personal healing is not for you alone, that it has a greater purpose: to free you to be a useful, effective instrument of the Divine for transforming all of humanity's quality of life.

Rising through and above the problems of your human life, you become part of the solution, and every life you touch is blessed. Be liberal in the use of your Matrix. Activating it causes two things to happen. You will become liberated from unnecessary burdens, and you will become free to act on the inspiration that lives within your heart. You will discover a profound sense of satisfaction. You will come to know an inner peace that is the result of participating and contributing to life to the best of your ability at any given moment. You will live your ordinary life in extraordinary ways.

Begin here. Start now. The Matrix will whir into motion, and moment-by-moment, it will lift you ever upward toward the high, lofty places, right where you belong.

Afterword

Before we conclude our work together, I'd like to briefly discuss the relationship between spiritual healing and the realms of physical, emotional, and mental health. I would also like to touch on spiritual health itself. Then I'd like to take one last look at our healing protocol before I send you on your way.

The Health Effects of Spiritual Healing

When I first started working in the Akashic Records, I had the idea that if I could just correctly manage the energy I found there, I would be relieved of all aches and pains. This has not proven to be the case! While I have enjoyed the gift of tremendous change and have seen my students experience such gifts as well, the actual outcomes of the work have invariably been different from my expectations.

Some people reap profound physical healing: a woman who came to me with a heart disorder, for example, no longer suffers from her illness and is medication-free. Personally, I have been relieved of emotional distress rooted in spiritual insecurity, a relief that centers on the pivotal notion of the trustworthy nature of Life and the spiritual forces present in it. Working in the Records in the ways I have described in this book, my awareness of the world as a safe place has grown exponentially, and my ability to see others as fundamentally good-hearted (even if not good-natured) has expanded far beyond my expectations. This shift in perception has made all the difference in my being able to relax and enjoy the goodness of Life.

I have seen students relinquish hardened resentments and find peace both within themselves and with those they had previously identified as adversaries. One woman arrived wanting to find out how to heal her brother from his greed; instead she released a burdensome feeling of jealousy and departed with a softened heart. Another transcended much inner torment as she recognized the futility of thinking that achieving an advanced academic degree—her third—could possibly win her father's approval. She did, however, go on to get that degree for her own reasons, which propelled her into a new and satisfying career.

Mine has been the great privilege of being with others as they recognized the part they play in their own dilemmas and set off with remarkable compassion on a new course toward peace and freedom. I have been there as people discovered within the Records the truth about their difficulties and became empowered to take healing actions on their own behalf. The issues I have seen brought to the Akashic Records have been of every type and variety: addictions, painful relationships, financial failure, physical distress—the entire array of human suffering. What has continually amazed me is that the solutions the Akashic Records suggest are always perfect for each unique individual and the exact circumstance he or she is facing.

This is how I know we are working with a higher wisdom, a greater consciousness—there is no other explanation for the tailor-made direction each person has received. While I have guided my students in their work, I certainly haven't supplied the answers myself, and previously they had been unable to discover the answers for themselves.

Some have not experienced the "miracle cure" they wished for—they have not been able to toss away their crutches and dance all night. Others experience only slight improvement in their health or circumstances. A man's back pain still comes and goes, but it's no longer constant; he's pleased with his progress but would appreciate total freedom from his pain. The woman who used to smoke a pack of cigarettes a day now smokes only at parties. She can enjoy herself on these occasions because she's free from the constant self-condemnation she used to bear. Another client longs to be a screen actress, but at the moment, she's glad to be in commercials and industrial films. Through her work in the Records, she came into contact with her Innermost Self and abandoned her career as an accounting clerk, knowing that this choice of jobs was not her truest self-expression. She's on her way.

Clearly, while spiritual healing through the Akashic Records can indeed have a dramatic effect on people's health—there can be radical transformations at every level—changes more often come gradually, and this gives us time and space to grow into them. Without exception, whether the manifestation is immediate or slow, a *shift in perception* occurs that sets the stage for changes we can ultimately see and measure. This shift in perception itself is the true healing, the spiritual healing that can affect the physical, emotional, and mental realms.

Once we no longer use our human imperfections as weapons against ourselves, the Light can move in and give us the relief we seek. As we gain the ability to see that the challenges we face can be used as launching pads into our future—as opposed to barricades between ourselves and our potential—we make that oh-so-necessary shift in perception. And then the Light enters and does its work. As we consider the possibility, for example, that our difficulties with the people in our lives are themselves the path to peace, we find the path taking shape before our very eyes. This consideration of expanded possibility—changing the way we *see* our difficulties—is itself the healing work.

Sound Spiritual Health

As we continue our work in the Records, transforming our ordinary wounds into sacred opportunities for transformation, we achieve greater spiritual health. All the effort we make to resolve everyday distress in the physical, emotional, and mental realms builds increasingly sound spiritual health, which in turn frees us to pursue improved health in all other areas.

We can consider our spiritual health sound when we are reasonably comfortable with this great paradox: none of us is the center of the universe, the point of origin for all life and power; rather, each of us is at the center of our *own* universe—and we are the convergence point through which all power of life flows. When our awareness is balanced in both truths, we find ourselves healthier than ever before—in all facets of our lives.

A Last Look at the Protocol

Now let's take a final look at the full protocol for healing through the Akashic Records. This is the series of four steps that emerged for me over the course of my decade-long work in the Records as a practical, effective method to meet the challenges of everyday life. Follow this protocol and you will experience transformation. Apply it to any condition whether physical, emotional, or mental. And, as you do so, remember that spiritual healing is about seeing life from a spiritual perspective, which is the perspective of wholeness and wellness. This is the level at which we can recognize the opportunity to know more love than ever before, no matter what our circumstances. Remember these steps:

1. Say "Of course you feel that way."
2. Acknowledge "These things happen."
3. Say "I am here for you. I will help you. We will find a solution."

4. Ask "How can this be good for me?"

Try it with me now—let's have one last practice session together. Think of something in your life that has been troubling you lately. Maybe you've just had the same argument with your spouse that you vowed to avoid. Perhaps you've lost your job. It's possible that you tried on your jeans from last fall and they no longer fit.

First, acknowledge how you feel. Say "Of course I'm upset. This is difficult. This is terrible."

Second, acknowledge what has happened. "These things happen. Many, many people have grappled with my issue. Right now it's my turn. I have done nothing wrong: this is part of being human—the hard part. I remember that I am good. I love myself, and I would never do anything to cause myself harm."

Third, offer yourself the same support a loving adult would to a child in distress. "I am here for you, no matter what happens. I will help you to the very best of my ability. Yes, this is a difficult situation, but I am here with you, and I will not leave you. You cannot scare me away. I will be here for you every moment of this journey. I am with you. I love you."

That brings us to the fourth step: "How is this good for me?" Or perhaps more accurately, "How could this *possibly* be good for me?"

At this point in our protocol, it is helpful to remind ourselves that all of life is conspiring to enable us to know our innate goodness. One of the great spiritual laws is "Seek and ye shall find." As you seek to discover how this repetitive failure, weight gain, job loss, or any other challenge could possibly be good for you, the seeking itself immediately increases the possibility that you will find the answer to that question. Our questions drive the journey. No one likes unemployment, or unproductive arguing, or other problems. It's true that you are fully entitled to the human experience with its full range of emotions including dislike, anger, and fear. But at this stage of the investigation, consider the possibility that this challenge is happening for your good, so you can come to know your essential goodness, even if you have absolutely no idea how to do that right now.

Sometimes it helps to pretend, suggesting to yourself that you know your problem arose for your good and you're just biding time until you can pinpoint the particulars. Keep raising the question, "How is this helping me to know my own goodness?" Stay in the present as much as possible and look for the answer. The answer to this question is the Light manifest in useful form: it will respond perfectly with a helpful solution to your problem. The best doctor for your condition, a new job, the resolution of tension in a relationship—these are all evidence of the practical presence and power of the Light. The answer, solution, or resolution is the Light in action.

Remember as you work with this protocol that it is not magic—it is a practical, and often gradual, approach to healing within the crucible of everyday human events. It will not dissolve your illness or your terrible predicament in an instant—though you may be surprised by how profoundly it works in your life. What it will certainly do is enable you to stop using your difficulties *against* yourself and begin to use them *for* yourself. This is a way to explore your situation that will not cause you greater trauma and pain. Rather, it allows you to be human and opens the path to your knowing the presence of the Divine under all circumstances. Remarkable!

Our Opportunity

Every age in history has its primary challenge, within which lies an opportunity. Our challenge today is to transform ourselves to recognize our Oneness: our unity with all people, all life, and the Divine Reality. We can use our difficulties to divide ourselves from one another *or* we can join together and unify with the awareness of our Oneness. The choice is ours. We are the people, and now is our time!

You now have ample tools, forged in the Light of Akasha, to help you make the most of this opportunity. Having taken the time and expended the effort to transform your relationship with your wounds to use them as points of power and paths to peace—to advance your growth and healing. Realizing that every hardship and injury you have sustained has offered you the chance to encounter the Divine Reality. With the spiritual means to explore your wounds—a way that does not limit you even further but instead enables you to expand outward and upward. In your capable hands is a healing system that will help you travel through the worst of your pain and beyond it into greater peace and freedom.

You are a magnificent and whole human being with finite aspects and infinite aspects—part human, part Divine. Live your life: own your experiences and allow them to propel you beyond all previous limitations. Reach inside, reach outside, give to and receive from Life. You are good—you have always been good. Love yourself and others. Dwell often in the safe, nurturing environment of the Akashic Records, the atmosphere of "Judge Not," "Fear Not," "Resist Not." Move toward life, and life will greet you with great enthusiasm. It will take you where you have always wanted to go.

Sharing this sacred journey with you has been an honor. I know you have been compelled by the urging of your soul to encounter this work and embark on this healing journey. I applaud you for hearing the call and responding courageously. You are on this path because you know that, as you become a peaceful, free, and happy person, you will become an agent for the very same transformation in the world. Now is the time for a glorious spiritual revolution, and together we are its agents. The radiant generosity and dedication you have shown toward your Self and all of life as you move toward spiritual healing through the Akashic Records are absolutely heroic and inspiring. It is wonderful to walk together toward greater Light and Truth. Sharing a commitment to know our souls even more, even better, we are advancing into a beautiful future here together on this planet, Earth.

Transforming the quality of life on Earth is a process with inner and outer aspects. Together we have explored the personal inner transformational experience with the aid of the eternal wisdom found in the Akashic Records. Through our work as individuals, we are each opening, expanding, and continually Ascending to higher levels of consciousness. Now we can unite, weaving together our individual points of light to create a single shining beam to illuminate the path for all.

Whether or not you and I ever meet in person, I know you are making a significant contribution to the realization of the magnificence of Life on our planet. When I feel love and acceptance, witnessing understanding and respect, observing people simply enjoying who they are in their everyday lives, I will know that you are participating. Each of us has a role to play in this spiritual revolution, and it begins now. You are on your way. Thank you for your courage, your commitment, and your compassion. I'll be looking for you out there. When we meet, I will recognize you by the light in your eyes, the warmth in your ways, and the joy in your spirit.

Until then,
Much love and many blessings,
Linda Howe

About the Author

Linda Howe is the leading expert in the field of Akashic Studies, specializing in the use of the Akashic Records for personal empowerment and consciousness development. Her first book, *How to Read the Akashic Records: Accessing the Archive of the Soul and Its Journey,* received the 2010 Coalition of Visionary Resources Award for the Best in Spirituality, Alternative Science, and Spirituality.

Linda has successfully taught thousands to work in the Records as a spiritual practice since 1996 and is the founder and director of the Center for Akashic Studies in Chicago, an organization dedicated to providing excellent training for those seeking to work in the Records. Widely regarded as a gifted teacher, Linda Howe is known for making spiritual ideas understandable and useful in the daily lives of her students, enabling them to experience the growth and transformation they seek. Linda is committed to supporting her students to recognize the Light within, to know their own soul more than ever before, and to demonstrate their essential goodness.

About Sounds True

Sounds True is a multimedia publisher whose mission is to inspire and support personal transformation and spiritual awakening. Founded in 1985 and located in Boulder, Colorado, we work with many of the leading spiritual teachers, thinkers, healers, and visionary artists of our time. We strive with every title to preserve the essential "living wisdom" of the author or artist. It is our goal to create products that not only provide information to a reader or listener, but that also embody the quality of a wisdom transmission.

For those seeking genuine transformation, Sounds True is your trusted partner. At SoundsTrue.com you will find a wealth of free resources to support your journey, including exclusive weekly audio interviews, free downloads, interactive learning tools, and other special savings on all our titles.

For a podcast interview between Linda Howe and Sounds True Publisher Tami Simon, please visit SoundsTrue.com/bonus/Linda_Howe_healing